MINIMALIST BUDGET

Save Money, Avoid Compulsive Spending, Learn Practical and Simple Budgeting Strategies, Money Management Skills, and Declutter Your Financial Life Using Minimalism Tools & Essentials

By
Jenifer Scott

TABLE OF CONTENTS

INTRODUCTION

At first glance, a minimalist budget sounds like it's all about less: spending less, doing less – less fun, less life?!

This book will show you that a minimalist budget is really about more – putting more simplicity into your finances, becoming more efficient at managing your spending, saving more money, getting more of what you want out of life.

Imagine your financial journey as a trip through an unfamiliar land. Do you have your sights set on a destination in the distance, and you are just not sure exactly how to get there? Or do you feel aimless and lost, walking in circles and returning to the same place over and over again? A minimalist budget provides a map to guide you on your financial voyage, helps to keep you on track in the most efficient way possible, and gives you guidance on how to avoid dangerous pitfalls and wasteful dead-ends. Using a minimalist budget allows you to take the complexity out of your financial life, see the big picture of where your money is going, and take control of what your money is doing for you.

There are many reasons you may be looking at this book. Perhaps you have always been conscious about spending and saving your money, and want to read about the methodology of doing it efficiently. Or perhaps you have had trouble with managing your spending, and want to get your financial life back on track. Maybe you make a six-figure income but just can't figure out where all your money is going every month.

No matter what your financial background and existing spending habits are, this book will show you what minimalist budgeting is and how to apply it to your goals and spending wants and needs. It will show you how to be persistent in your budgeting approach, even if you encounter setbacks and life changes.

With a minimalist budget, you can still have things that bring you convenience, comfort, and happiness. But the key to the minimalist budget approach is intentionality in how and when you buy things. By applying the concepts described in this book and being honest with yourself, you can take control of your possessions and spending. You can direct your resources meaningfully and with intent, helping you achieve your financial goals.

CHAPTER 1

Minimalist Budget Essentials: Entering The Minimalist Mindset

What a Minimalist Budget is and What it's Not

To many people, a minimalist budget sounds like an extreme form of being frugal. They imagine someone eating canned foods and sleeping on a mattress on the floor, spending their days clipping coupons. In fact, a minimalist budget is a very different concept from being frugal.

A minimalist budget is about streamlining your finances, prioritizing your financial goals, and having a good knowledge and control of your income and expenses. It's about being able to direct money toward the things that are most important to you. It's about reducing clutter in how you approach your finances and your possessions.

It's important to keep in mind that a minimalist budget does not necessarily imply spending less money. You can still choose to have expensive things, even luxury items, as long as they have a purpose and meaning in your life. However, a minimalist budget is likely to encourage you to spend less. Once you carefully account for your spending and prioritize your goals, you will be more efficient at using your money toward what you really want in life, instead of wasting your resources on trivial things.

A minimalist budget will help you to shift your priorities away from acquiring things just because they are a good deal, and toward getting things and experiences that you really value in life. What you value may not necessarily be less expensive, but you will not clutter your life with things that are not important. For example, instead of owning twenty pairs of shoes, all of which you got on sale for a really good deal, you might have just a few high-quality pairs that you really like, and which fulfill specific purposes in your life.

Living on a minimalist budget is about being efficient with your money and focusing on just the essentials in your financial approach. This differentiates it from being thrifty or frugal. A thrifty person looks for the best deals, uses coupons, accumulates points and rewards on their credit cards. Trying to get the best deal is commendable, but without a minimalist budget mindset, it's still easy to waste money by buying things just because they are on sale. This is where a minimalist budget will help you. You can prioritize your goals, avoid impulse purchases, and make the most out of your time and money.

How a Minimalist Budget Can Improve Your Life

Simply put, a minimalist budget can help you get freedom and simplicity into your life. By using intentionality to direct what your money is being spent on, you can stop wasting money on things that don't matter. You can direct your cash flow toward the things you really want in life, in the short term, and in the long term.

A lot of people are stuck in a cycle of earning money and spending it. If they work hard and earn more money, they just end up spending more money, because they start wanting more expensive things. They never actually feel content with what they already have, and it's hard for them to "get ahead" in life because they are hardly aware of where their money is being spent. Our society is very focused on acquisition as the source of happiness, and it's very easy to fall into this pattern.

A minimalist budget can stop the acquisition cycle and make you content and in control of your finances (and your life). At the core, we still have a hunter-gatherer mindset – we like to look for things! In modern life, this often materializes into shopping, (sometimes without a particular objective, just to see what's on sale or to find a good deal), browsing Craigslist or eBay to see if there is anything we might like to buy, looking at shopping catalogs, and doing other activities that involve just looking for something to buy.

A minimalist budget can free you from the cycle of searching for something to buy, getting that something, briefly experiencing either fulfillment or regret, and then moving on to looking for something else to buy. This cycle does not actually make you happy – it's a waste of your time and money. Inside, you know this, because while you feel excited looking for something to buy or anticipating a purchase, after you actually acquire that something, you do not feel that happy. Even if it's something you have wanted for a long time, you feel a slight sense of being let down, a little disappointed (and in some cases, full-on regret!) The only thing you can think of doing to make yourself feel better is to look for something else to buy next – perhaps accessories for your recent purchase, or just the next acquisition.

On the other hand, living on a minimalist budget can stop this wasteful purchasing cycle. It will show you ways to feel content and fulfilled by guiding you to your goals and letting you bring things into your life that actually have meaning and significance. By using a minimalist budget, you can streamline your purchasing process, focus on getting only the things you really need, and work on the financial goals that really matter in your life.

Another important benefit that a minimalist budget offers is less stress. For many people, worrying about paying their bills or other obligations can be a constant struggle. Ironically, this can be the same people who frequently make impulse purchases. Many relationships are strongly affected by money management or lack of it. Money is one of the leading reasons for arguments for couples. Relationships between parents and kids (of all ages) can be put under stress from differences in purchasing and entitlement viewpoints.

This is where a minimalist budget can help you. If you do not start controlling your money, your money ends up controlling you and negatively affecting your relationships with others. Using your minimalist budget, you can take control of your financial life. You can stop unnecessary spending so that your bills are lower to start with, and then you can get rid of your debt. You can plan a future that focuses on mindful spending and adding value to your life and your relationships.

Your Mindset and Attitude are at the Core of Minimalist Budget **Success**

Before focusing on the budgeting and planning aspects of minimalism, you have to get into the minimalist mindset. If you are not in the right mindset, you will find yourself trying to cheat yourself: see if you can slide that fancy latte in under the grocery expenses, borrowing money from your emergency fund for that shirt that's on sale because it's such a good deal and you can't miss it! (Even though you have dozens of other shirts). If you are not really focusing on your financial goals and priorities, a minimalist budget will feel like it's working against you, preventing you from enjoying life and getting the things you want. Eventually, you will just decide that the minimalist budget is not for you and give up. You will miss out on the great opportunities that the minimalist budget approach offers: to make you fulfilled, efficient with your spending, and goal-oriented.

If you have the appropriate mindset, you will understand that your minimalist budget is helping you to be more efficient, moving you toward your goals, the important things in life, making you happier.

Much like yoga or other mindful activities, getting into and being in a minimalist mindset is a "practice" – a continuous process rather than something you achieve and set aside. If you are used to spending money on trivial things, the initial minimalist practice will feel challenging – like stretching or trying to do physical activity after you have been sedentary for a long time. But the more you practice being in the minimalist mindset, the more second nature it becomes, and the more you will enjoy actually putting your minimalist budget thoughts and ideas into reality. Eventually, your old habits of mindless spending will seem very wasteful to you. The "thrill" of looking for something to buy will be replaced with contentment, and knowing that you are doing something that's useful for your life.

4

The good news is since you are reading this book, you are already well on your way to incorporating the minimalist mindset into your life. Chances are, you have already begun to understand that spending money is not making you happy. Conversely, it's probably making your life worse! Perhaps you have recognized the cycle of looking for something to buy and the lack of lasting fulfillment that follows the purchase, and want to end it. Or you have allowed your spending to create financial issues in your life, and you would like to get back on the right track.

As a part of your minimalist mindset practice, direct your thoughts toward the reason you are considering living on a minimalist budget. Think about the buying cycle you have been in, and where it got you, both from a financial perspective and from the perspective of how it has made you feel in the long-term. As you are faced with temptations and opportunities to purchase things, return your thoughts to this and ask yourself to make a new decision this time, a decision that will get you out of the mindless spending cycle.

An important part of your minimalist approach is letting go of comparing yourself to others. Many of our purchases, both impulse ones and planned ones, are caused by us comparing our possessions to those of our friends, relatives, co-workers, and neighbors. We often give little thought to whether a particular object will really bring value or happiness into our lives. Instead, we focus on how we measure up to others – with our gadgets, vacations, cars, and many other things. We want to feel normal, to fit in, or to be better than others.

Wanting to fit in is normal, but keep your own happiness in mind the next time you consider a purchase that's based on keeping up with others. Ask yourself if you are acquiring something that will add value to your life, make things easier for you, or make you happy. There will always be someone in your life who can spend more money than you – that's a competition you cannot win, and you don't need to, to be happy.

It's also important to let go of entitlement. Many advertisements focus on convincing you that you "deserve" their product. Do you not deserve a new car, the latest phone, an island vacation? The marketing strategy works, because most people feel like they deserve nice things – they are not bad people, and perhaps they have been through a hardship that makes them feel more "deserving." However, this is not a helpful mindset to have, as you can always say you deserve more, and you can never have enough with the "*do I deserve this?*" approach. A more helpful strategy is to ask yourself "*do I need this?*" "*will it make me happier?*" "*how does it fit into my budget compared to other things I value?*"

Money is a resource, and you have to make active decisions about using this resource. If your impulse purchasing is frequently fueled by the thought that you deserve something, make that "*do I deserve it?*" into "*can I afford it?*" and think about the things you are making tradeoffs with by making that purchase.

Living on a minimalist budget is as much about the journey as the destination. It's not just about getting to the goal you set for yourself – it's about living a life where you feel good about your financial behavior and efficiency. You won't miss your wasteful spending, because you just won't feel like you need to spend money to be happy.

As you practice living with a minimalist mindset, return your thoughts to these concepts frequently – letting go of entitlement and comparisons, seeking contentment and long-term fulfillment in life, and not just a spending distraction. The following chapters will discuss in more detail how you can use this mindset to create a minimalist budget and use it to improve your life.

End of Chapter Exercise

Select one of the following quotes related to minimalism:

- ☐ *"Simplicity is the ultimate sophistication."* —Leonardo da Vinci
- ☐ *"The secret of happiness, you see, is not found in seeking more, but in developing the capacity to enjoy less."* —Socrates
- ☐ *"Too many people spend money they haven't earned, to buy things they don't want, to impress people they don't like."* —Will Rogers
- ☐ *"You have succeeded in life when all you really want is only what you really need."* —Vernon Howard
- ☐ *"There are two ways to be rich: One is by acquiring much, and the other is by desiring little."* – Jackie French Koller
- ☐ *"Nothing is enough for the man to whom enough is too little."* – Epicurus

Recall the quote the next time you go shopping.

CHAPTER 2
Defining Goals And Priorities

This chapter will show you how to set priorities that are in line with a minimalist budget mindset. We will take a look at how a minimalist budget can be used to achieve specific goals, such as eliminating debt or building up savings.

Set Your Priorities

Your minimalist budget should support what is important to you, so it's critical to examine and understand your own goals and motivations. Your goals and motivations may change over time, and this is ok because your budget can change over time as well. Your priorities could be about paying off debt, saving money for a specific purchase, or by a specific timeframe or age, retiring at a certain age, giving money to your children or a charity.

Keep in mind that each dollar you spend on something else works against this goal. It does not mean you should not spend money – we all need basic things like food and shelter, and we want to live our life fully. However, examine each purchase decision while weighing it against your goals and priorities. Is the fancy coffee or the sweater on sale more important than your goals? Your answer in each case will depend on many factors, but being in the minimalist mindset will help you make the right decision.

If you are not sure how to set your goal, consider the following ideas. You may pick something directly from the list, or a combination of these items, or a modified version of these that fit your own circumstances:

- Pay off debt: This can be credit card debt, student loans, hospital bills, money you owe to friends or family, a car loan, etc. Debt can be very stressful to deal with.
- Do not spend more than what your income is: This goal can work in conjunction with paying off debt. If your spending habits continually exceed your income, you will always find yourself in debt in the future, even if you pay off all your current debt. This goal is a good step toward setting up for an even better one if you are not doing this yet.
- Put away money into savings (emergency funds, special expenses, retirement accounts)
- Regularly donate a portion of your income to a charity or organization that you are passionate about or that has a special significance in your life.
- Save up for a special gift or event, for yourself or someone you love (graduation, wedding, honeymoon, a vacation, a big purchase that means a lot to you).

These are just some of the financial priorities that may be important to you.

Considerations for Setting Your Financial Priorities

In setting your financial priorities, you have to consider what your own life circumstances are, what feels right to you. You will be more successful at sticking to your minimalist budget if your goal is something that really calls to you, something you've wanted for a long time, or is passionate about. If you are working toward the financial goal that really matters to you, every day using your minimalist budget will make you feel good about yourself. Every trivial purchase you forgo will actually make you feel happy because you are trading off this purchase with something much more valuable to you.

It's important to be realistic about the goal or goals that you set for yourself. If you are used to a lifestyle where you allow yourself to have anything on a whim, making a drastic change can make you feel demotivated. Pick goals that you can honestly commit yourself to and try living on a budget that supports these goals.

Another aspect to consider during the process of setting your financial priorities is the topic of ownership. Concentrate on owning, not borrowing, when acquiring things. Avoid stretching your budget by seeing what cars or toys you can lease, or what you can afford as payments. Be realistic about the lifestyle you can really afford.

Also, consider the difference between buying things and experiences. Things, by themselves, do not actually make us happy. Experiences are really what we remember, even if they are enabled by things that we bought. Reflect on your goals and what experiences are important to you. Can they happen without the same level of spending? For example, instead of getting a pool for "family time," are there other experiences that will bond you as a family and still be a fun and memorable time without the expense? If you like a certain sport, do you have to have the latest and most expensive equipment to enjoy the sport itself? Or can you spend less on the equipment and go on a vacation involving this sport instead? Examine your priorities and determine where, instead of buying things, you can focus your money and effort on experiences.

As you work on defining your goals and priorities, limit yourself to only one or two goals to work on at a time. Tracking progress toward many goals at the same time can get complex. There is also the matter of how to store money toward many goals, while at the same time keeping your financial life simple. Selecting many goals will split your savings contribution to each goal to a small amount, and you may get discouraged because little progress will be made toward any one goal. Remember that a minimalist budget should make your life less complex and your goals easier to attain. Your goals should be selected in the spirit of that notion.

Finding Motivation

Your motivation for living on a minimalist budget may be very straightforward – you have a large amount of debt, and you want to pay it off, or a future expense you want to save up for, or perhaps you just want to simplify your life. But sometimes the financial goal by itself may not be enough to prevent you from an impulse purchase and make you stick to your budget. It's important to identify a long-term motivation that you can think about when tempted to spend money, something that will motivate you even after your debt is paid off.

Here is a thought-starting list of motivations you can use. See if any of these apply to you and motivate you to spend less on trivial things. Can you come up with other motivations that really move you, something that really matters to you?

- Retire early
- Quit your current job and get another one that may pay less, but involves something you really want to do
- Being able to help your parents or your children with their finances
- Travel the world
- Help others in need

As you can see, these motivations are goals in a way, but they are less specific and involve long timeframes – years, decades, or even your lifetime. Your motivations can be just one thing, or many things, as long as you focus on something specific that you really care about accomplishing. Your motivations are in the background of your financial goals and priorities. These are the things that will inspire you to stick to your budget, to avoid that compulsive purchase, to keep trying to accomplish your financial goals even if you have a setback.

The process for incorporating your financial priorities into your minimalist budget will be explained in the next chapter.

End of Chapter Exercise

Select a goal that you have not achieved yet.

- ☐ Paid off all credit card debt, student loan debt, car loan, and current bills
- ☐ Saved up one month's worth of living expenses
- ☐ Saved up six months' worth of living expenses
- ☐ Started to put away money for retirement
- ☐ Saved up enough money to retire comfortably

Now, set your sights on your goal!

CHAPTER 3
Budgeting And Money Management Strategies

This chapter discusses the approach to creating and managing a minimalist budget. The methods and concepts in this chapter demonstrate how minimalism is applied to budgeting in a practical way. We will also take a look at behaviors and practices that facilitate minimalist budgeting.

For the purpose of creating your own minimalist budget using these guidelines, it is easiest to consider your income and expenses on a monthly basis, as many bills and other obligations occur at a monthly frequency. The examples in this book typically show how budgeting strategies apply to a month's worth of income and expenses. However, the same techniques and concepts can be applied over a span of days, weeks, months, and years.

Analyze Your Income

Your minimalist budget starts with knowing how much money you have coming in.

If you have a regular income (a job or another source of money that pays a relatively constant amount at regular intervals), use the net monthly amount you get as the input to your budget. "Net" means the actual sum of money you can deposit into a bank after all applicable tax and social security deductions.

If you work seasonally or have work where the income varies predictably over the course of the year (the tourism industry or fishing enterprises are good examples of this), your monthly income for budgeting purposes should be the average over the year. To get the monthly average, divide your net annual (yearly) income by 12 months.

If the money you have coming in is not consistent, and it's hard to predict how it may vary in the future (for example, if your pay is based on commissions), utilize the "worst-case" amount you may get – for example, the lowest monthly pay you have received over the past year.

Do not count on any money you may or may not get in the future – raises, bonuses, promotions, inheritances, winning the lottery – all these can be incorporated into your minimalist budget if and when they materialize, but not before then.

Of course, if your income does change significantly (up or down), your minimalist budget needs to be adjusted to comprehend the change.

In the medium and long-term, you can also consider what else can be done to increase your income:

- In your current job, focus on what actually makes you money. If you are a commissioned, hourly, or self-employed worker, this means making the most of your available working hours and earning opportunities. If you are a salaried employee, reflect on what earns you raises and bonuses and put your energy into activities that are tied to getting you that additional money. Don't get caught up in spending your days on tasks that your employer does not care about, or you can delegate those tasks to others.

- You can also acquire a side job or applying for a higher-paying position. Ask yourself if you are making good use of your free time now and if this time can be directed toward earning money. There are many online resources (Craigslist jobs and gigs, indeed.com) where you can look for part-time jobs that fit your skill set and availability.
- One source of money that is very well aligned with the minimalist strategy is to review your possessions and sell things that are cluttering your life. Think of what you own and how often you use these things, and how much happiness they bring you. Can you turn them into cash so that they can be used toward your goals and things that actually matter in your life? Online resources such as Craigslist or eBay can be good ways to make some money on the things you don't have use for.

Analyze Your Current Spending and Estimate Future Expenses

Understanding where your money is going to is a critical input into your minimalist budget. Make a list of what you have spent for the past several months and group purchases and expenses into categories. If you use a credit card, credit card statements often organize your purchases into categories for you, or you can use the following list when organizing what you have spent.

Some of your expenses will be fixed – that is, they don't change month to month. Examples of fixed expenses are:

- Rent
- Mortgage
- Car loan
- Insurance premium payment

Other expenses are variable – that is, they can vary month to month, either depending on external factors or choices that you make:

- Utilities (these may vary with your usage and outside temperature)
- Cable/phone bill/internet bill/other service subscriptions
- Groceries
- Transportation
- Clothes and personal care
- Medical expenses

- Entertainment
- Travel
- Gifts
- Other categories that apply to you (kids' activities, pets, hobbies, fitness, etc.)

After listing and organizing your expenses, do a quality check. Do your last month's expenses and savings contributions actually add up to your income? If you used a credit or debit card to pay, it's easy to account for all the expenses (or at least, the places where you spend the money). If you used cash, not only do you have to keep track of your bank or ATM cash withdrawals, but you also have to keep a diligent record on how this cash was spent.

As you evaluate your expenses, many of them should not surprise you – if you have a mortgage, this is the amount you have signed up for. Most of your expenses for groceries, transportation, and service subscriptions will probably be more or less constant every month.

However, watch out for spending amounts and categories that surprise you: were you aware of how much you were spending on eating out or new clothes every month? Is this level of spending in line with your long-term goals and priorities? Establishing awareness of your financial behavior and weighing it against what you really want to accomplish with your money is critical to creating and following a minimalist budget approach.

Now, you have to estimate your future expenses in each category. Estimating your fixed expenses is easy – this is the same amount you have spent in the past. If you anticipate a change (for example, if you know your rent payment will increase next month), then use the new amount.

Estimating variable expenses will take some judgment and decision-making on your part. If the expense varies more or less randomly, or due to events that you can't reliably predict, you can calculate an average monthly spending amount for each category for future planning purposes. Calculating an average is easy: you add up the amounts spent in each month that you tracked in the past and divide by the number of months. For example, if in the last 3 months you have spent $400, $600, and $500 on groceries, the average per month is ($400 + $600 + $500) divided by 3 months, or $1500 / 3 = $500 on average for groceries per month.

Some variable expenses may vary predictably. For example, if you live somewhere where the weather is really hot in the summer, your utility bill may be higher in the summer months due to using the air conditioner more. You can estimate the expenses that vary predictably by examining what you have spent in the past and projecting that pattern into the future.

After completing your expense analysis, you should have a list of expense categories and an estimated expense amount for each category. The next section will show you how to use this information to make a budget. For the purpose of deciding how much to allocate to variable expenses, start out by making a budget for the next month. Once you can do this, you can repeat the process for future months, where your variable expenses may be different. Later in the chapter, you will also learn how to incorporate expenses that don't happen monthly, and how to review and maintain your budget so that it is up to date.

Create Your Minimalist Budget

Now it's time to create an efficient and streamlined spending plan – a minimalist budget. You will use your financial priorities from Chapter 2, together with your income and spending list from earlier in this chapter. The process for making a budget involves creating a monthly expense list that you commit yourself to. This plan has to work with your obligations and life priorities.

We will go through the process using an example, and you can follow through with your own inputs.

First, list your monthly net income:

Income	$2000

Next, list the monthly expenses you are obligated to right now. This list will vary person to person, but typically this is what you must pay no matter what (at least in the short term, without selling your house or making drastic changes in your life). Things like your mortgage or rent, utilities, and car payments are in this category. Many of these expenses will typically be fixed, but some – utilities, for example – may be variable:

Income	$2000	Rent	$400
		Utilities	$100
		Car Payment	$200

Now, take your net monthly income and subtract these must-have monthly expenses. How much do you have left? This is the amount that your budget will use toward achieving your financial goals, and also toward your discretionary spending.

In the example above, the remaining amount is $2000 - $400 - $100 - $200 = $1300.

Now, this is where the financial goals you have defined earlier come into play and become specific amounts of money. If your goal is to pay off debt or save a specific amount of money every month, decide what this monthly amount needs to be and make this money an entry into your expenses list.

This amount will depend on several factors, such as your minimum debt payment, how much you owe or want to save in total, and over how much time. Chapter 4 contains a lot of detailed guidance for determining your savings and debt repayment amounts. As a good starting point or general guideline, allocate 20% of your net income to your financial goal. In our example, 20% of $2000 is $400:

Income	$2000	Rent	$400
		Utilities	$100
		Car Payment	$200
		Savings	$400

Keep in mind that accomplishing some financial goals may take time, and you have to plan how your budget will be affected by them over the years. If you are planning a career or job change, or anticipate life changes that may affect your ability to contribute to your financial goal (having a child, for example), your plan needs to comprehend this. For example, you may want to set a more aggressive savings rate for now, if in the future, you will have other expenses.

Next, you create a budget plan for everything else on your list. It helps to arrange the list by priority, specific to your needs and preferences. This way, if you have to make tradeoffs and make decisions on where to decrease from your current level of spending, you can focus on areas that are lower in priority. The prioritization list will really be about your own values and circumstances in life. For example, different people will put different priorities on things like having a nice meal at a restaurant, having a gym membership, sending their kids to private school, drinking high-quality coffee, etc. None of these are life necessities, but they are things that may be valuable to some people and not to others.

A lot of the expenses in your budget will be variable – that is, you did not spend the same exact amount of money on them in the past, and you have to estimate how much to allocate to them in the future. Review the previous section in this chapter if you are not sure how much to allocate to each category.

Now calculate your total expenses. This is just the sum of all the expense categories on your list, including your savings goal. The total expenses will be either greater than your income, less than your income, or equal to your income.

Review the resulting budget:

- If your total expenses are greater than your income: Where are you willing to make some compromises and reduce your variable expenses? You have to ask yourself whether your past spending in each category is in line with your goals and values. Did your past purchases in each category result in things in your life that were valuable and useful to you? Remember that you cannot change your fixed expenses. Your savings goal should not be changed either. As long as you have made a realistic target, you need to be committed to it. Your strategy is to reduce your

variable expenses, especially the areas where you can exercise discretion in how you spend the money.
- If your total expenses are less than your income – you have some breathing room in your budget! Allocate this extra money toward your savings.
- If your total expenses are equal to your income, then you have made a budget!

Here is how we continue our example:

Income	$2000	Rent	$400
		Utilities	$100
		Car Payment	$200
		Savings	$400
		Phone / Internet	$100
		Groceries	$300
		Clothes	$200
		Entertainment	$200
		Travel	$200
		Total Expenses	$2100

Uh-oh, did you notice that our planned spending exceeds our income? Through this process, keep in mind that this is a minimalist budget – while you may value or like some things, can you live without them or find alternatives that do not cost as much? Many things that we do every day only clutter our lives with activities and spending but do not really provide anything lasting or meaningful. For each expense category you have on your list, ask yourself whether this item is really helping you to live a meaningful life that is in line with your values and long-term goals. In our example, you can decide that you don't need $200 worth of new clothes every month and can do with $100. Or perhaps you can reduce your entertainment and travel budgets. In the end, you should have a plan where your savings goal is still intact, and your monthly spending plan does not exceed your income:

Income	$2000	Rent	$400
		Utilities	$100
		Car Payment	$200
		Savings	$400
		Phone / Internet	$100
		Groceries	$300
		Clothes	$100
		Entertainment	$200
		Travel	$200
		Total Expenses	$2000

The bonus chapter at the end of this book will give you ideas for how to make your money go further in various categories of spending.

How to Approach Expenses That Do Not Happen Monthly

Your budget is a plan for your monthly income and expenses, but it also has to comprehend items that happen less regularly, or only during certain times of the year but not every month. Examples of this are property taxes, holiday gift expenses, vacations, etc. Keep in mind that these are expenses that you plan - this does not include unexpected expenses and financial setbacks, which are discussed in chapter 5.

One of the most straightforward ways to comprehend irregularly occurring expenses into your monthly budget is to calculate the total you need for the expense, and then divide by the number of months from now when you will need this sum of money. For example, if you are anticipating that your property taxes are $1000 and they are due in 5 months, then you need to save $200 each month from now on for this expense. As you are planning farther ahead, you can start calculating the total that you will need over the course of the year, and then just divide by 12 months, similar to how the concept of a variable income was handled.

Planning expenses that do not happen monthly, or happen at irregular intervals, are critical to your minimalist budget. Forecasting how much these expenses will cost will prevent you from continuously trying to compensate for these items and falling behind on your monthly savings and debt repayment plan. At a very minimum, your minimalist budget needs to prevent you from spending more than what you make. Failing to account for incidental expenses is a big pitfall that can wreak havoc on your spending and make you feel like you are not in control of your money.

As you incorporate planned special expenses, like vacations and big-ticket purchases into your budget, you can also see more clearly how they affect your monthly spending and tradeoffs with other usages of your money. Keeping these expenses in mind for budget planning may make you re-evaluate the necessity of these purchases.

There are several items to keep in mind with irregularly-occurring planned expenses:

One consideration is how to "store" the amount that you save monthly for these expenses.

This will depend on personal preference:

- With a cash based approach, you can withdraw the money each month as cash. Of course, there are possible downsides to this as concerning the secure storage of this money and potentially missing out on earned interest, but this is an option that may fit some situations.

- With online banking, you can store the monthly allocation to a savings account. Regularly check your math to make sure the amount in the account corresponds with the total you should have for all the irregular expenses. It is best not to leave the money allocated toward your irregular expenses mixed inside the account you use toward your monthly expenses.

In addition to making a plan for saving for irregular expenses, carefully consider the overall necessity of each expense in this category with your minimalist mindset. Property tax amounts are a given, as long as you are living in the same house. However, items such as vacations, gifts, and other optional expenses should be given a lot of thought.

The primary consideration is not necessarily "How little can I spend?" but rather, "How can I direct my money more effectively with what I am trying to accomplish?" Consider the last few trips and vacations and gift-giving sessions. Was your previous approach a good use of your money, did it make you and those around you happy? Is there a more financially effective approach that will also make you happy? The answer to this is highly personal and will depend on many individual factors.

We are all familiar with the concept that simple gifts that were made or acquired with a lot of thoughts are the memorable ones. Or that sometimes you can have just as much fun on a "staycation" (that's a vacation where you stay at home) as on a real vacation, as long as you are doing what you enjoy. These concepts may or may not apply to your personal situation, or perhaps you already have some of your own ideas about how you can make expenses like these more financially efficient and meaningful. Your minimalist mindset practice will guide you to how best to make your overall financial goals compatible with these expenses.

Simplify Your Financial Life

A very important part of living on a minimalist budget is decluttering your financial life. As you recall, minimalism is not about spending as little as possible and using a jumble of cashback incentives and rewards. Instead, reducing the number of credit cards and bank accounts, you have will help you track your expenses and simplify your life.

The minimalist budget accounts are consist of:
- One debit or credit card for purchases
- One checking account, where your income gets deposited and where the money for your monthly expenses are stored
- One savings account, where you have your emergency savings and money for non-monthly expenses
- Retirement accounts (401k, IRAs, etc.) will depend on your particular job and life situation, but in general, a simplicity in the management of retirement accounts is also helpful in tracking your money. Some people are hesitant to invest in a retirement

account simply because they don't want to deal with picking investment options, rebalancing their portfolio, and other money management things that may sound complex or intimidating. Fortunately, retirement investing has some very straightforward options:

- o For a really simple approach, choose a target year fund. These funds automatically allocate your contributions toward different types of investments to be appropriate for when you are going to need the money. The allocation is typically more aggressive and growth-oriented if you have a long time before you need the money, and more conservative and income-oriented if you are retiring soon (and/or are expecting to make withdrawals soon).

  To pick a target year fund, just select your approximate retirement year, or the year when you think you will need to start withdrawing the funds. Because there is some work associated with the automatic rebalancing of investment allocations, target year funds typically have somewhat higher management fees than index funds (more on those next), but considering how hands-off this option is, the fees are quite reasonable at most investment firms.

- o Another very simple investment approach is to invest in index funds. Index funds are designed to track a specific subset (index) of stocks, funds, and other investments – for example, the S&P 500. Index funds simplify your investment choices and tax returns over picking individual stocks, or even individual non-index funds. They typically have low management fees, as they just track the average performance of other investments. You can just pick a handful of index funds to have an allocation among stocks and bonds that is appropriate for your age (search for "age appropriate investment allocation" online for more on this aspect).

- o If you have multiple 401k and other retirement account plans accumulated from changing jobs, consolidate them into a single self-directed IRA account. This will give you the benefit of being able to see how your money is invested all from just one portal, which facilitates adjusting the overall distribution in your portfolio.

In addition to simplifying your accounts, it is also important to simplify how you access your statements and other financial information. Whenever possible, sign up for e-statements – they are easy to access and store. You can dispose of your paper statements and other documentation – it will physically declutter your life. Be sure to exercise appropriate precautions in how you dispose of confidential and sensitive information (something that contains your account numbers or social security numbers), and how you choose and store passwords for your electronic logins.

When you get an e-statement or a bill, pay it right away – this will avoid you accidentally forgetting to pay it, which usually incurs penalties and fees. If you are waiting for a paycheck before you can pay a bill, for most credit cards, you can schedule a payment to occur in the future, before the due date.

Combining some or all of your recurring debt obligations into one loan can be a great way to simplify the way you perceive and manage your debt. Getting multiple bills throughout the month can be a stressful thing in itself, not to mention the complexity of managing the various due dates, amounts, and agencies to pay the money to. In addition, if you are currently paying a high-interest rate, you can save money by consolidating the loans under a lower rate. You can check on consolidated loan interest rates at your own bank, check rates from other banks online, or investigate if you can transfer the debt to one of your existing loans that have a favorable interest rate.

Regularly Review Your Minimalist Budget versus Reality

With a minimalist budget approach, it is critical to be very aware of your income, your spending, your savings, and your progress toward your goals. Schedule a regular weekly time, where you review your financial performance. If you have a partner with whom you share your financial goals, include them in this review as well. The weekly cadence is important, as it gives you enough time to identify if you are off course and still meet your monthly goals.

At each review, ask yourself the following items:
- Is my monthly income what I expected, or have there been unexpected changes? If something has changed, is this a one-time occurrence or do I need to adjust my monthly budget permanently?
- How am I doing with setting aside or paying money toward my long-term financial goal? Are there unexpected factors that are preventing me from following my plan, and how can I incorporate them into my monthly plan for the future?
- Am I staying on track with my monthly expenses for this month?
- How was my performance versus my budget last month, did I stay on track?
- Very importantly, look for additional ways to cut out unnecessary spending in your life. This should be a continuous process, but as

you review your actual performance versus your budget, you may see some areas where you can direct your focus.

At first, the review process may seem boring or difficult, especially if you are not a numbers person. However, you will be amazed at how satisfying it is to look at the evidence that you are following your plan and making your goals into reality. Regular budget performance reviews will also allow you to see how factors that are outside of your control (a tax hike, fuel prices) are affecting your expenses and adjust your plans to take these changes into account.

It is also important to regularly review your accounts online – that includes things like credit card activity, bank deposits, and withdrawals. With online banking, this can easily be done in minutes. Do a quick check on your accounts every few days, which will flag any unexpected activity for you and prevent surprises in the future.

As you document expenses and plan future spending, it's important to be as exact as possible with your numbers. Don't "guesstimate" what you might have spent on groceries or your night out. Check your credit card statement or your receipts and write down the specific amount of money involved. Remember that estimating is likely what got you to seek using a minimalist budget in the first place – you want to have better control and understanding of your finances.

End of Chapter Exercise

Select the amount of money that most closely approximates what you have spent on eating out at restaurants last month (including fast food):

- ☐ $0
- ☐ $50
- ☐ $100
- ☐ $200
- ☐ $300
- ☐ $400
- ☐ $500
- ☐ $1000+

Did know the answer off the top of your head or did you have to look it up?

CHAPTER 4
Minimalist Budget Tools

In the previous chapter, we examined the overall minimalist budgeting methodology, as well as the methods to implement and execute your minimalist budget. Now, we will take a look at some specific tools and techniques associated with minimalist budgeting, and how you can stay organized and focused on your goals. We will also look at some specific budgeting strategies in more detail so that you can choose an approach that makes the most sense to you.

Payment Automation

Automating payments for your loans and savings deposits can greatly simplify your financial life, and simplicity is at the core of using a minimalist budget. Most financial institutions will allow you (in fact, they prefer you too!) to make regular automatic payments and deposits. If you have trouble to get yourself to put away money every month toward savings and end up spending it, payment automation is a trick you can use to "hide" money from yourself, so it's not even there for you to spend it.

For debt payments, make sure to automate at least the minimum required payment and more if you can afford it (see the next section for more on how to make decisions in this area, and how this should balance with allocating your savings).

For your credit card, make sure to pay the full statement balance every month, not just the minimum, to avoid high-interest rates.

For mortgage, rent, and lease payments, and everything else that has a set amount due every month, the simple strategy is to just set the automated payment to the amount due (unless you are also trying to prepay your mortgage).

Automating payments gives you several advantages:

- It prevents you from accidentally forgetting to pay your debt or credit card balance, which in most cases triggers fees and/or high-interest rates.
- It also makes it easier for your mind to think of the payments as a given, not something that's optional so that you don't even contemplate using that money and adjust your spending plan as if the pre-allocated money was not even there. If you automate a reasonable amount to go to your savings every month, pretty soon you will not even miss the money, as you will be used to living without it. The savings will accumulate in your bank account all on their own. We will discuss strategies for determining how much to put into savings later in this chapter.

Reverse Budgeting

Payment automation is closely tied to the reverse budgeting method. With reverse budgeting, you set aside money for specific purposes as your top priority, and spend what's left as you wish. Instead of deciding in advance what you will spend on each category of expenses, which can be tedious and can discourage people from doing any budgeting at all, you focus on just your goals on obligations.

For example, if you have $2000 as your net income every month, with a reverse budgeting strategy you can decide that you want to put away 20% of your income ($400) toward savings. You automate this payment and use the money you have remaining ($1600) toward everything else in your life.

Reverse budgeting is a great way to build savings, especially when combined with automatic contributions to a designated account. As you may have noticed, the budget-building strategy used in Chapter 3 is also tied to reverse budgeting – we figured out our net income, designated money to basic living expenses, and then allocated a specific amount of money to our financial goal.

In addition to a savings goal, you can also incorporate your basic living expenses and your minimum debt obligations into your reverse budgeting allocation. Set this amount aside, and you don't have to plan or budget how you spend the rest of the money.

With reverse budgeting, you need to have a reliable system of separating the money you set aside for your savings from your discretionary money. This means the money you are setting aside needs to go into a separate savings account, while your discretionary money stays in your checking account. As an alternative, you can withdraw your discretionary money as cash every month, while keeping your savings in the bank.

The downside of reverse budgeting is that you can still engage in making impulsive purchases and overspend in some categories because you are not examining closely where your discretionary money is going. If you have some extra money coming in, you are likely to spend it on something discretionary instead of putting the money toward repaying your debt faster, or toward your long-term financial goals. As with any budgeting method, your intention of being a responsible spender and saver is critical to your financial success.

The Zero-Based Budget

This budgeting approach has a somewhat technical-sounding name, but the concept itself is very simple: your income minus your expenses should equal to zero. It does sound very simple, but many people fail to properly account for this concept and end up in debt.

Making a zero-based budget uses the same overall strategy as what we have discussed in the previous chapter. First, you write down your income, obligations, savings target, and various categories of expenses. Then, you make a plan where resources, goals, and priorities come together – which usually involves some tradeoffs.

While the reserve budgeting approach gave you some discretionary money for which you did not need to have any specific plans, with a zero-based budget, you are accounting where every dollar from your income goes to. It is a more rigid system, where you have to stay organized in how you track your spending. However, it gives you the advantage of deciding where each dollar would be most useful – making extra payments on debt obligations, saving up for a vacation – as opposed to just letting you spend any extra money. The reverse budgeting method is very much in line with the minimalist mindset because it requires you to plan and spend purposefully.

The 50/20/30 Budget

The 50/20/30 budget (also known as the 50/20/30 rule) guides your budgeting strategy by giving you the relative proportions of spending and saving that you can follow. This rule can help to keep your budget balanced and your financial goals on track. To follow the 50/20/30 rule, make the following spending and saving allocations when creating your minimalist budget:

- 50% of your net income is allocated to the absolute necessities that you cannot avoid paying. This is typically your rent or mortgage payment, utility bills, and the absolute minimum you can spend on food, transportation, and other must-have items. This category is your highest priority. Be very critical of your spending habits when including items into this category! Just because you are used to buying something, it does not mean you cannot live without it.

  If you find that your absolute minimum necessities consistently exceed 50% of your income, then you need to make a lifestyle change. This may include downsizing your house, getting rid of a car payment, or moving to a less expensive area. Examine what your necessary expenses consist of, and ask yourself how you can reduce them. There are a few ideas on this in the bonus chapter at the end of this book.

- 20% of your net income is allocated toward savings. If you have debt obligations, the money is allocated toward debt repayment – and as much savings as you have left over. After repaying debt, the money goes toward retirement savings, emergency funds, saving for near-term and long-term expenses, and other money allocation toward the future. This category is your second-highest priority after paying for the absolute necessities in life.

If you have debt obligations, little or no emergency funds, and little or no retirement savings, you have to make some choices about the relative distribution of your money toward these savings types. Here are some ideas about how to approach this:

Debt: Of course, you have to make minimum debt payments. Depending on the interest rate, you may want to pay back more than the minimum payment so you can pay back the loan quicker and focus on contributing to your savings. If the interest rate is sufficiently high, you may never be able to pay back the debt without making higher than minimum payments. Using information from your loan provider (or you can search for a "debt repayment calculator" online), determine how long it will take you to pay back the loan at your current rate of repayment and how much interest you will end up paying. If you have extra money in the 20% savings category, consider paying more toward your debt to shorten the repayment duration and reduce the amount of interest you will pay.

Emergency savings: As a general rule, you should have 6 months' worth of living expenses saved for emergencies. This includes the absolute necessities category, plus minimum obligations on debts. Build up your emergency savings to this amount as soon as you can, while making at least minimum debt payments.

Retirement savings: The importance of saving for retirement early cannot be overemphasized. You can find many articles and examples that illustrate what a great advantage an early start of retirement savings gives you (search for "saving for retirement early vs. later" online). Even as you are repaying debt and contributing to your emergency funds, consider putting away at least a little toward long-term and retirement accounts. This is especially important if your employer matches some of your contributions – make sure to contribute at least the amount to take full advantage of the matching – it's free money.

- 30% of your net income is allocated to discretionary expenses. Discretionary means that the expense is optional, and you can decide how you want to spend this money. This includes categories such as entertainment, vacations, and any other purchases that are not essential to your survival. This category has the lowest priority. If you have an unexpected expense or a financial setback that impacts your ability to contribute to the absolute essentials or savings and debt repayment, the extra money can come out of this category.

In some cases, the line between necessities and optional expenses can be blurred. For example, most of us have a smartphone and can't imagine effectively functioning without it (though, we actually can, unless you need your phone to perform your job). Or it can be as silly as saying to yourself, "I can't survive without those new shoes or that fancy cup of coffee." Be mindful of the instances where you convince yourself that something is a necessity.

The good news is that using the 50/20/30 approach automatically makes you decide on the tradeoffs among your optional expenses. As long as you are honest with yourself that you can possibly live without a given expense, you can list all the things you would like to spend money on and choose among them. You can even change the allocation over time for some variety – for example, spend more on eating out and entertainment one month, and buy yourself some new clothes or gadget next month. The choice is yours, as long as you keep it within the 30% allocation.

For example:

Income	$2000	Necessities (50%)	$1000
		Savings (20%)	$400
		Discretional (30%)	$600

Since the 50/20/30 rule is based on percentages of your income, you can apply it no matter whether you live on a big salary and have a lot of expenses, or you do not have that much money coming in, and you live frugally. The important thing to keep in mind is that it's up to you to decide what you consider a necessity in life and what is optional and allocate your budget accordingly. Do not underestimate the importance of the 30% savings category, and do not "borrow" from it or buy things telling yourself that they are "an investment." Your future self will thank you for being diligent and properly contributing to that 30% savings category, as this is the budget allocation that lets you get ahead in life.

Here are some downsides to the 50/20/30 budget:

- First, sometimes it can be hard to separate wants from needs: which expense goes into the necessities category, and which goes to the discretionary category. You need to eat food, but do you need a steak and a salad for dinner, or would anything more expensive than ramen noodles be an indulgence?
- Another downside is that the allocation can cause you to be wasteful. If you have extra money left over from your 30% discretionary category, you will feel tempted to just spend it instead of saving it, because you have technically met all your savings and debt repayment obligations for the month.

The 50/20/30 budget can be a very useful guideline, but it does require you to closely track the allocation of your purchases into the necessity and the discretionary spending categories.

The 80/20 Budget

The 80/20 budget is a simpler alternative to the 50/20/30 budget. The concepts are similar, but with the 80/20 budget, you do not have to track necessities separately from your discretionary spending. You simply put away 20% of your income into savings, and the remaining 80% is yours to spend on everything that you want and need.

As with the 50/20/30 approach, automatic withdrawals into a savings account is critical for the 80/20 approach, so you are not tempted to spend that 20% and learn to live without it.

You also have to be mindful of how you spend that 80% of your income. This amount still needs to cover basic necessities and obligations. You don't have to budget for various spending categories, but you need to be disciplined enough to prioritize where spending your money is essential (for example, your rent payment) and which expenses are not as important.

The 60/40 Budget

The 60/40 budget (also known as the 60% budget) is another very simple method you can use to keep your expense allocation on track. The 60/40 approach puts an emphasis on expenses that you have commitments to, whether they are wants or needs. It also gives you a good structure for allocating your savings into different categories. Here is how it works:

- 60% of your income is allocated to existing commitments: mortgage or rent, service subscriptions. Your basic living expenses for food and transportation go into this category as well. If you find that the sum of your expenses in this category exceeds 60% of your income, then you have made too many commitments. For ideas of how to deal with this issue, review the minimalist budget ideas for recurring expenses in the bonus chapter at the end of this book.
- 40% of your income is allocated to savings and discretionary spending. The breakdown is as follows:
  - 10% is for short-term savings. This includes money for unexpected expenses, vacation savings, gifts, and other expenses for the near future. This money should be easily accessible, though not combined into the same account as your monthly expenses.
  - 10% is for long-term savings. This includes big purchases like cars or down payment on a house and money for big

medical bills and emergencies. This money is typically invested, but still accessible.

- o 10% is for retirement savings. This money goes into your 401k or IRA account, within applicable contribution limits.
- o 10% is completely discretionary – you can spend it on anything you want.

The 60/40 budget is a great way to guide your savings allocations while at the same time, ensuring that your basic living expenses are covered.

If you have a lot of debt (outside of a mortgage obligation), you can temporarily use contributions, 10% for long-term savings and 10% for retirement savings to pay down the debt. The following sections explore the various approaches to debt repayment.

Paying Off Debt with the "Snowball" Method

Debt obligations can be very stressful. Especially if you have multiple loans, it's easy to start feeling like you are drowning in bills, statements, and due dates, and not making any real progress toward repaying any of it.

The snowball method is all about building momentum in your progress toward repaying your debt obligations. Just like with building a snowball, you start out small and work toward big results.

The overall idea behind the method is to pay off your smallest debts first, build encouragement and momentum, and go on to tackle the big debts. It's a mental technique to show yourself that you can take control of your financial life. Here is how the snowball method works, step by step:

- First, review your budget to make sure you have enough money to cover the minimum payment for every one of your debt obligations.
- Arrange the debt obligations by size, from smallest to largest. Disregard the interest rate on each debt with this method.
- Allocate an additional amount of money, on top of your minimum obligations, that you will use for debt repayment.
- Every month, use the additional debt payment amount toward your smallest debt obligation. Only pay the minimum payment on the other debts.
- Once you pay off your smallest debt, use the money you paid on it (the minimum plus the extra allocation) toward the next smallest debt.

For example, let's say you have four debts, with the following minimum payments:

Debt	Total Owed	Minimum Payment

Hospital bill	$300	$50
Credit card	$1000	$100
Car loan	$5000	$150
Student loan	$10000	$200

You have allocated the money needed to make the minimum payments ($500), and in addition, you are able to contribute an extra $100 per month toward debt repayment.

Using the snowball method, you would make the minimum payments on each loan, plus put the extra $100 toward the hospital bill ($150 total toward the hospital bill per month). In a few months, the hospital bill is paid off, and you put that money you paid toward the hospital bill ($150 per month) as an extra payment toward your credit card ($100 minimum payment + $150 extra = $250 per month toward the credit card). Continue this until all the debts are paid off.

The advantage of the snowball method is that it lets you demonstrate to yourself that you can make tangible advancements in paying off your debt. It's the most effective way to quickly reduce the number of bills coming in, so you stop feeling overwhelmed and start feeling like you are making real progress toward debt management.

The downside of the snowball method, as you may have guessed, is that it does not take into account the interest rate on the loans so you may be paying a higher rate for a longer period of time. This is a valid argument, but remember that the snowball method is about building motivation and encouragement. If you prioritize paying for the loans with the highest interest rate, you may be saving some money on interest, but the progress you are making may seem less tangible. Without seeing real progress, you may lose motivation and stop contributing the extra money toward debt repayment, thus negating any savings related to interest rates.

Paying Off Debt with the "Avalanche" Method

Unlike the snowball method of repaying debt, the avalanche method does not necessarily give you small victories or encouragements up front. Instead, it focuses on making debt repayment as efficient as possible by having you pay off debt with the highest interest rate first.

If you have read about the snowball method and just can't imagine yourself not putting your money toward the debt with the highest interest rate, then use the avalanche method instead. You have to be patient and methodical, sticking to your extra payment strategy even if a year later you are still paying on all of your loans.

Taking our earlier example, we arrange the debt by interest rate this time:

Debt	Total Owed	Minimum Payment	Interest Rate
Credit card	$1000	$100	10%
Car loan	$5000	$150	6%

| Hospital bill | $300 | $50 | 5% |
| Student loan | $10000 | $200 | 3% |

In this example, you also have $100 extra to spend toward debt repayment each month. With the avalanche method, you would pay the minimum on all the loans, plus an extra $100 on the credit card bill each month. It would take you longer than with the snowball method to pay off a debt completely, but you will save money on the interest you are paying for this debt.

The avalanche method takes discipline and may not bring you a sense of accomplishment as fast as the snowball method. However, it's rooted in solid financial logic and can save you money if you commit yourself to it.

Paying Off Debt with the "Snowflake" Method

The snowflake method utilizes small amounts of savings or extra cash you find yourself with to chip away at your debt. You still pay the minimum obligations on all your debts, and in addition look for opportunities, no matter how small, to save money and contribute it to debt repayment.

The advantage of the snowflake method is that it does not require rigid planning for allocating extra money in your budget toward debt repayment. You only allocate the minimum payment amounts in your planning phase. After this, you have to be diligent throughout the month to find additional money to contribute toward debt repayment. This can be little things, like not buying your usual latte on the way to work, having a garage sale, or selling something on Craigslist.

Although each contribution may be small, a consistent and diligent approach to looking for little bits of extra money in your daily life can add up to respectable chunks of cash over the course of the month.

In choosing which debt to contribute the extra money to, you can combine the snowflake method with either the snowball or avalanche methods.

Pay with Cash

In today's world, purchases are greatly simplified with debit and credit cards, not to mention the ability to pay through an app on your phone or smartwatch. Impulse purchases are all too easy, as you only see the transactions on your statements and probably don't feel any less poor right after completing the purchase.

On the other hand, getting and using cash can be a bother, as you physically have to go to an ATM or a bank, and then store the cash and carry it around.

Make the difficulty of dealing with cash work to your advantage, and use the cash for all in-person purchases. Even the trouble of having to take out the cash from your account can help to prevent the purchase. And as you hand over the cash, physically parting with money can lead you to be more prudent in future purchasing decisions because you feel the impact immediately.

You can use cash for most every day, in-person purchases. For larger purchases that may require buyer protection or a refund, use a credit card.

The Envelope System

The envelope system can work hand in hand with the cash approach described above. The approach is simple: each month, leave enough money in your checking account to pay for your current bills, debt obligations, and savings target, and take out the rest as cash. Next, list the categories of your monthly expenses and allocate an amount to each category, as shown in Chapter 3. Assign an envelope to each category, and put the cash amount that you have allocated to that category in each envelope. Each month, you can only spend the amount in the envelope for each category. You can refill the envelopes either once a month, or after each paycheck.

As a variation on the envelope system, you can also use clips (with some labels), which may be easier to manage in your wallet or purse than envelopes. As another variation, you can also use a small accordion folder and assign a pocket in the folder for each category.

For online purchases, you can use a "virtual envelope." Write down your total allowed spending amount for the category on an envelope (or a piece of paper). When you make a purchase online, subtract the amount you just spent from your allowed amount. When you get to zero, you are not allowed to buy online anymore.

If you make several shopping trips per month (let's say, for groceries), only take the amount of cash you intend to spend on the individual trip, not the whole month. That way, you don't talk yourself into splurging on something on the first trip, while finding yourself with insufficient cash to buy even the basics at the end of the month. If you get to the checkout and you don't have enough cash to pay for everything, put some items back – that's prioritizing in real time!

The envelope system requires discipline and the ability to be honest with yourself. No borrowing from other envelopes! If you are really craving some fast food but you don't have your "restaurants/fun" envelope with you, then you cannot spend on fast food because you did not plan for it. If you are making a purchase that involves multiple categories (let's say, if you are buying some fuel and a beverage at a gas station), you have to be diligent and take the cash out of the appropriate envelopes. Admittedly, this can get logistically challenging, especially considering you also have to put the correct change back into the correct envelope, but the logistics become easier to handle with practice.

The envelope system approach really encourages you to plan ahead and to be frugal with your spending. Once your grocery envelope runs out of money, you're done buying groceries for the month – knowing this can prevent you from wasting food or buying unnecessary items at the store. Once your fuel envelope runs out of money – well, you better plan ahead and walk or carpool when you can, and don't make unnecessary trips.

If you are sharing your budget and the envelope system with your significant other, you can either split the allocations or have your own set of envelopes, or in some cases; one partner may control the envelopes for specific categories. It is very important to agree on a plan ahead of time and to stick to this plan. If something unexpected comes up (you ran out of money for a category), you will need to discuss and agree upon a strategy with your partner.

If you have some money left over in an envelope at the end of the month, this is great news. You can reward yourself (put it into your fun/entertainment category), or keep it in the same category and save it toward the next month. You can also take the extra money and apply it to paying down debt, or toward your savings goal. If there is a category where you never find yourself overspending and always have money left over, consider "graduating" that category to being eligible for credit card usage or combine the category with another one.

The envelope system makes it impossible to overspend if you are diligent at using it and are being honest with yourself. The approach is great for habitual overspenders and impulsive buyers — you physically cannot spend more than you what planned on! The system also lets you easily identify areas where you may be consistently budgeting too little or too much money. It's important to review your monthly performance versus your envelope system and make adjustments to your plan or your lifestyle as needed. The good news is, while it's easy to review credit card purchases once a month when you get your statement and spend frivolously until then, the envelope system makes you evaluate your spending decisions in real time.

The "One In, One Out" Rule

The One In, One Out rule can help you to control your spending and curb your acquisition of "stuff." This rule can be applied to non-consumable goods, such as clothes, shoes, cars, etc. The concept is that when you buy something, you have to get rid of something that you own in that category. If you buy a new pair of shoes, get rid of a pair you already have. For compulsive shoppers, this can be a great tool in questioning the necessity of the purchase.

Another way to use the rule is that you have to use up or wear out the item before getting a new one. This ensures that you have made maximum use of your current possessions before moving on and getting something new.

The No Spending Day

The no spending day approach can be a great tool for trying out living without your daily spending "needs," without committing to quitting them outright.

Schedule a regular "no spending day" once a week.

For example, you can forgo that cup of fancy latte, bring leftovers for lunch instead of buying a meal, or walk when you would have normally called a ride-sharing service. Chances are, you will see how easy it is to give up a regular expense in your life, and make new habits that do not involve spending.

You can take the "no spending day" further and make it into a "no spending week," or "no spending month," where you do not allow yourself to make any discretionary purchases just for that time period. It can be a very empowering experiment – and lets you save a little (or a lot of) money once in a while.

Budget Tracking Methods

There are several ways to approach your budget planning and tracking. If you are not a math or spreadsheet person – don't worry, the key to minimalist budgeting is simplicity.

- The "classic" paper and pen approach. This method may be a little "old-fashioned," but some people may prefer the simple and concrete way this system lets them record and access their budgeting information, rather than having the numbers in a computer or online. Sometimes a piece of paper with numbers on it just feels more "real" than digits on an electronic screen. If you do go with this approach, make sure to have an organized system for recording and storing your information. You can use a journal or notepad (get one with lines, as opposed to just blank pages), or have a folder with pockets where you file your records.

- You can also do your financial tracking electronically, which makes it easy to quickly find and update information, make copies of it, and store it in a place where you can easily assess it on the go – on your phone or laptop (By contrast, paper versions can get lost or damaged, and they are not as convenient to make copies of).

  There are several excellent online tools that let you plan and track your budget. Simply search for "budget tracking tool" or "budget tracking app" online and check out the selection to see which one might best suit your preferences. Some apps are more or less online spreadsheets, where you can enter your income, planned versus actual expenses, savings, and debt payments. Others (for example, mint.com) offer the ability to consolidate viewing all your financial accounts into one app and send you alerts about upcoming bills and unusual account activity.

- You can also track your budget with a simple spreadsheet on your computer, using Excel or a similar program. The examples shown in this book can be done quickly and easily using a spreadsheet program, or even just a Word or Notepad type of application.

The most important attributes of your budgeting method should involve being easy to access, read, and update. Your budgeting method has to work for you. If just the thought of getting out your budget and reviewing it gives you a headache, try a simpler approach. Fancy expensive budgeting software won't help you if you tend to avoid using it because of its complexity.

In this chapter, we have looked at a number of tools and methods to help you organize your minimalist budget, pay down debt, and facilitate your finance management. In the next chapter, we'll take a look at how to address issues when working with a minimalist budget.

End of Chapter Exercise

Imagine you can sell back anything you have purchased (and still own) for its original purchase price. The only catch is that you have to deposit your refund into an emergency fund so you can't just replace the things you sell back with a newer version.

Look around to see what you are willing to sell back (don't forget to check the closets). Pick the amount that most closely resembles the maximum total "refund" that you can get for your emergency fund:

- □ $0 (not willing to return anything)
- □ $100
- □ $500
- □ $1000
- □ $5000
- □ $10,000+

How does this amount compare to your real-life emergency fund?

CHAPTER 5

Dealing With Compulsive Spending, Setbacks, And Unexpected Expenses

Budget-related setbacks generally fall into one of two categories: those we absolutely have no control over, like natural disasters, and those we failed to control. There is also a gray area in between, based on considerations of how much control we actually have over ourselves.

This chapter will help you to analyze your setbacks, adjust your budget and your mindset, and plan for the future so that you can control the setbacks you cause yourself, and the setbacks that you cannot control do not affect you as negatively.

Expect the Unexpected

Some financial setbacks are certainly not anything you can prevent or control – accidents happen, things break, our friends and family ask us for help. Sometimes, all these things happen at the same time, and your rainy day becomes a perfect storm! However, you can do some "preventative maintenance" in life to help lessen the impact of the unexpected expenses:

- Examine your "unexpected" expenses for patterns: Just because you have not planned for an expense, it does not mean that it was not predictable. Doctor and dentist visits, home and car maintenance, and property taxes are items that are likely to happen sooner or later, and you should include planning for those into your regular budget allocation. Chapter 3 explains how to approach expenses that do not happen monthly, and Chapter 4 shows you the various approaches you can take to incorporate that allocation into your budget.

- Have an emergency fund: Even if you already have many financial obligations, putting away just a small amount every month can be extremely helpful. Review Chapter 4 for how you can allocate an amount toward this goal. It's important to remember that this is not your "I ran out of money, and I feel like buying something" fund. While the emergency fund should be easy to access, it should only be used for extreme cases such as medical emergencies or natural disasters.

- Do some preventative maintenance: This applies to your home, your car, and your own body. Repairing a faucet is a lot less expensive than repairing water damage that a broken faucet can cause. Leading a healthy lifestyle is a lot less expensive than dealing with the illnesses associated with things like overeating, smoking, not exercising, and not washing your hands. There is a reason that cars come with maintenance schedules – things are likely to go wrong if you don't follow them.

- Get insured: Car insurance, health insurance, homeowners insurance, even pet health insurances are tools you can use to mitigate the financial impact when disaster strikes. The coverage should be appropriate for shielding you from the costs that you can't pay for yourself. You can also "self-insure" yourself for some expenses by putting away money into an emergency fund as if you were paying an insurance premium.

- Look for alternatives: Some expenses can be significantly lowered or delayed until you can pay for them. If you have an unexpected medical bill (this applies to veterinary bills too), you can negotiate with the hospital to pay a lower amount or to pay in installments. If you have to make a trip, you can check into using frequent flyer miles or drive instead of flying. If you have to make car or house repairs, you can consider doing the work yourself if you have the necessary skill set, or you can ask someone you know to do it in exchange for help with something you can do.

The Psychology of Overspending

We may not be able to control natural disasters, but studies show that 40-80% of purchases are impulse buys. For spending decisions, we do have some control over, it's important to examine what causes us to make the decision to buy. The reasons can be very personal, and they may be rooted deeply in our experiences and natural tendencies. However, we can group the reasons into general categories that can help you understand the background for your own overspending:

- Influence from others and social pressure: Humans are social creatures, and much of our behavior is tied to interacting with others. Our purchases can be caused by us comparing ourselves to others, the fear of missing out on the fun or the good deals that other people are enjoying and getting involved in herd mentality about the necessity of certain purchases. There is also what we consider social obligations: gift reciprocity and gift-giving occasions (where some competition can occur as well).

- Shopping momentum: Once you have purchased what you intended, your mindset tends to remain open to making acquisitions. It felt good to set a buying goal and accomplishing it, so naturally, we want to do it again. This is where budgeting and being deliberate with deciding what you acquire is very critical.

- Stress and external factors affecting our disposition: Stress can make us avoid purchasing decisions, so we end up buying more than we intended. Stress can also make us feel like we deserve a treat or something extra because we are under pressure, so we go shopping and buy ourselves something to improve our mood. Positive moods can affect us too, as we can be overly optimistic about our finances. It's important to recognize when you are susceptible to make poor buying decisions. Avoid going shopping when you are stressed out, make good plans, and stick to them.

- Living in the present: Normally, the concept of living in the present is a good thing, but when making purchasing decisions, we tend to put a lot of emphasis on how we feel at the moment as opposed to planning for the future. Making a purchase has the ability to give us instant gratification, and we may fail to consider how our actions will affect us in the future.

- Unrealistic expectations: Sometimes, we fail to be realistic about the amount of money we allocate to the various categories in our budget. We make a budget that's very restrictive compared to the lifestyle we are accustomed to, and we get discouraged when trying to adhere to our own plans. It's important that your minimalist budget is sufficient to cover the basic necessities and also allows you to stay inspired and motivated by your plans.

- Money abstraction: The way we earn, store, and spend money today allows us the option never actually to see or handle cash. Modern payment methods such as credit cards, electronic payment transfers, and the ability to pay with your watch or phone make life convenient. However, they also make money less "real" – money becomes just some numbers; you don't have to part with anything when you make a purchase. The repercussions for overspending are delayed, and there is nothing to discourage you from overspending at the time of the actual purchase.

While this information may help you understand why you are spending more money than you intend to, the following sections contain suggestions for taking control of your spending. Remember that living with a minimalist budget is largely about mindfulness, about doing things in a purposeful way. While you may not be able to change your natural tendencies and impulses, understanding yourself is critical to modifying your behavior.

Embrace Money and Embrace Yourself

No one is perfect. Even with the best of plans, we tend to forget, procrastinate, lose our focus, and get demotivated once in a while. This is normal.

Keeping in mind that our hunter-gatherer mindset is what drives us to look for things to purchase, the habit of spending money on unnecessary things can be hard to break. In addition, once in a while, all of us experience financial setbacks that are out of our control.

It's important to examine how you view money and your relationship with it.

Avoid negative thoughts about money – it seems to be attracted to people who like it, and it tends to run away from people who don't like it. Money in itself is not "evil," as some people think, but it can cause financial problems if not handled properly. Money is an opportunity.

As they say, "money can't buy happiness" (or love), but it can certainly enable us to do the things that make us happy. To make your money work for you, you have to realize that managing money is about tradeoffs. You can choose how to direct the money you have to accomplish the most happiness. You can also choose to make additional money, so you have additional options.

When you make mistakes with money, remember that people can change. If you have certain habits, it's not necessarily who you are. With the right mindset, you can change your habits and behave differently, more in line with what you value and who you want to be.

If you find yourself unable to avoid impulse purchases, do not get discouraged. When faced with the next challenge, remind yourself about the feeling of regret in your past purchasing experience. Use this as a motivation to avoid making the purchase, and thus not feel this regret again.

It's helpful to write down the reasons that have caused you to make an impulsive purchase, not pay your bills on time, or fail to allocate your planned amount toward savings. Once you have your reasons on paper, review the list for patterns. Are there factors that keep happening over and over that cause the problem, and how can you minimize or avoid the influence of those factors? Even if the reasons are random or seemingly out of your control, think of ways you might account for their unpredictability in the future. Can you put away a little money toward the unexpected every month, or avoid situations that might lead to fate wreaking havoc on your financial plans?

Distinguish Between Needs and Wants

Be very questioning about every purchase. Ask yourself if what you already have is enough to keep you happy. Can you possibly do without the item that you are considering? Getting more is not necessarily better; it just fills your life with meaningless things. Some things can be enjoyable, even useful, but still not qualify as a necessity.

Focus on Simplicity and Function

With that said, a minimalist budget is not meant to make your life difficult – quite the opposite, you should focus your money on things that make your life simpler. If you forgo buying a microwave and a dishwasher because you can live without them, going without those things (for some) actually may make life more complex. You may spend more time cooking and cleaning, and when you don't feel like dealing with that, you will just go out to eat and spend more money, negating the savings of not buying the appliances.

Your possessions should be a balance of meeting your essential needs, simplicity, and bringing enjoyment and satisfaction into your life.

Avoid Temptations and Plan Your Purchases

Some of the time, our urge to buy something is triggered by a specific situation – driving or walking by a store where you like to shop, getting a catalog in the mail, or receiving an email about a sale. There is a reason grocery stores often put candy in the checkout lane – no one really needs candy, but seeing it can trigger the urge to buy it, for a lot of people.

- Examine what triggers your urge to buy unnecessary things and remove these temptations from your life.
- Unsubscribe from sale notifications, catalogs, store emails, and other things people send you to get you to buy things.
- Avoid shopping malls and other places where you will be tempted to make unplanned purchases. Do not go to the store "just to see what's on sale." You will end up buying something you do not need.
- Unfollow items on social media that focus on reviewing and promoting things to buy.
- As much as feasible, limit your exposure to advertisements and other media information that is trying to get you to buy or invest in something. As we watch TV or even drive by billboards, we are bombarded by all kinds of suggestions about how you should spend your money (and what a good deal it is). Ignore these distractions and focus on your goals and priorities.

Always plan your purchases in advance. To avoid impulse buying, walk away as soon as you give yourself any of the following reasons to buy something:

- It's on sale, for a limited time
- I might need it in the future
- I deserve to have one of these
- Someone else I know has this

None of these are good reasons to acquire something – it is a waste of your money. Follow these steps once you decide that a purchase is truly necessary:

- Research the specific item you want to buy. Look at the product reviews and specifications to make sure it fits your needs.
- Consider alternatives – something you already own or can purchase. Are there other items or variations of this product that can fulfill your needs and be more cost-effective? Ask yourself if

you like everything about this item. Do you really love it, or can you wait until you can find a better variant?

- Consider ownership cost (will this item make you buy more things, like accessories or require maintenance or other additional expenses?)
- Consider additional aspects of owning this product, other than cost. How often will you really use it? Where will you keep it so it will not clutter your life? Do you have to get rid of something else first before you have room for this new item?
- Research how much the item costs. Is it possible to acquire it online at a lower cost? Is getting this item in used condition an option? Are there windows of time when buying this item may be less expensive than usual? (Seasonal sales are a good example of this).
- Determine the price you can acquire the item for and allocate the cost into your budget. In some cases, the allocation may be a savings amount over months or even years, and in other cases, this can be a one-time expense in your monthly budget.
- Give yourself some time to think it over. This is the key to avoiding an impulse purchase. Wait at least a day from the time you have decided to make a purchase before going ahead and proceeding with the transaction. If you find yourself in a situation where you say to yourself *"Well, I'm here now, so I might as well buy it,"* this is a sign that you have not planned this purchase in advance and likely don't actually need this item. The longer you can wait before purchasing, the better. You will be surprised how many times you will reconsider the purchase after walking away from the store, or after living without it for a few days or weeks and realizing that you don't actually need it in your life. You will actually feel a sense of relief that you did not buy it!
- After completing the proper considerations, make an informed and purposeful purchase!

By using this process, you are making sure that the things you acquire are really what you want, that they will have room in your life and won't clutter it, that they are useful and have good value. This is shopping like a minimalist.

Form New Habits

At first, making a decision not to make an impulse purchase will be difficult. Your mind has made well-worn "tracks" in your decision-making landscape, and its tendency is to direct you to buy things! However, as you make new decisions not to purchase something, your mind will become more used to this line of thinking – making new "tracks," in a way. This will not happen overnight, or just by you reading this book – change takes time, and behavior changes take a mindful effort.

After some time practicing the minimalist mindset, you will notice that you actually feel more content and satisfied if you decide not to buy something. The decision not to make an impulse purchase will become easier, until it is second nature, and you are actively seeking out other ways to make your financial life, or your life in general, more efficient and less wasteful.

Forming and breaking habits can take time, but the more you do something, the easier it is to get yourself to do it next time. Practice making the right decisions for your budget, and you will become better at it.

There is a nice bonus in getting used to living with less: you become more appreciative of what you do have in your life. If you are used to quickly giving in to your own whims and wishes, your frequent acquisitions mean less and less to you. On the other hand, giving up something and only having it occasionally makes it into something worth appreciating! Do this with something you are used to giving yourself "as a treat" frequently: this could be a fancy latte on the way to work, a glass of wine with dinner, buying new outfits, or electronics. Rather than depriving yourself of the treat entirely, reduce the frequency - if you have a fancy latte every day on the way to work, only allow yourself to buy it once a week. You will notice that something which you used to take for granted is now really special and fun! As part of human nature, we are equipped to really appreciate good things if we receive them in moderation, not all the time. Take advantage of this, and maximize your enjoyment of things through the minimalist approach.

Distract Yourself and Keep an Open Mind

As a strategy, distract yourself with an activity that does not involve spending money. Go for a walk or schedule some quality time with friends and family. There are many things you can do for free, or very inexpensively, that can bring joy into your life. Keep in mind that spending money does not directly lead to happiness.

Of course, what is fun to one person may not be that much fun to another. In order to expand your own options of simple and inexpensive ways to enjoy your life, spend a week writing down at least one thing per day which you would enjoy doing, and which costs very little or no money (including transportation). This activity also should not involve looking for things to buy. Here are some ideas for the list:

- Go for a hike on a nearby trail.
- Look at books at a local library, or check out what books you already own.

- Check for free books on Amazon (many classic books are free, and the reason they are "classic" is that many people have liked them through the ages)
- Volunteer for a cause that you care about.
- Schedule some family time – play some games.
- See a local high school sports game.

There are many distractions and fun things to do that do not involve spending much money. See the "Entertainment" section of the bonus chapter in this book for additional ideas on this topic.

You can also distract yourself by thinking of achieving your financial motivation (from Chapter 1). Won't it be nice once you are finally able to put your dreams and aspirations into action? Imagine yourself in the act of enjoying what you have planned – traveling, helping others, retiring in comfort.

Learn from Experience and Adjust to Life Changes

Remember to regularly review and adjust your minimalist budget to comprehend any life changes. Check how frequently you have expenses that you think of as unexpected or covered by special circumstances. Can you anticipate these expenses better in the future, and either find a way to prevent them or incorporate them into your financial planning?

If you anticipate a future expense that either temporarily or permanently will affect your budget (for example, the birth of a child or the need for a new car), review its impact on your finances in advance. Can you start putting away money into savings now to avoid a larger adjustment later? Identify some areas where your spending is discretionary and which can be easily adjusted when needed.

Learn from your experience as you utilize your minimalist budget in real life. If you make an impulsive purchase, think back to the sequence of events that led you to buy it. Did you go shopping for one thing and ended up buying something else? Try to avoid similar situations in the future – when you go shopping, make a very specific list of the things you want to buy and the amount of money you want to spend on them. Also think carefully about how the impulse purchase has made you feel immediately after, as well as how it's making you feel now. Did it make your life better? Are there other things you would have rather had instead of having made that purchase? Return to the reflection on your post-purchase feelings the next time you are faced with buying something. Chances are, if you have not planned on buying it before, then you do not need it.

Your attitude toward money and your confidence in yourself are important for getting you back on track when you experience financial setbacks. Learning to live on a minimalist budget will take time and adjustment. The reward of living a simple and empowered financial life is worth the work.

Impulse Buying Prevention Tricks

So you have made a budget, organized your wants and needs and planned out your purchases, but when you actually go to the store, you still end up buying things you have not planned on. You know that you want to declutter your life and live simply, but you just can't pass up a good deal, and those purchases are wreaking havoc on your budget.

Here are some additional tricks and techniques to try to curb your unplanned purchases:

- Set a minimum for every purchase that's not in your budget. For example, for purchases over $20, you have to wait 24 hours before you can buy it. For purchases over $100, you have to wait a week. For purchases over $1000, you have to wait a month. You can adjust the amounts to fit your budget.
- Make a deal with someone so that every time you make an impulse purchase, you will give them the amount of money you have spent on the purchase. All of a sudden, good deals stop being so good because you have to pay double!
- When going to a store, bring only enough cash with you to buy what you have planned on. Don't take any debit or credit cards along.
- Calculate how many hours of your work the item is worth. Even if you work for a salary, on commissions, or are self-employed, chances are you know roughly how much you make per hour while working. Convert the cost of the item you are considering to hours of your work and see if you still feel that it's worth that much of your effort.
- Invoke the "one in, one out rule." Think of an item you already own that's similar to what you are considering purchasing and commit to getting rid of this item.
- Even if you are looking at the item in person, pull up online reviews of it (you can use Google or Amazon for this). Go right to the negative reviews and ask yourself if you still like the item as much.

End of Chapter Exercise

Imagine that due to industry downsizing, you have just learned that your net income will be reduced by 10% starting next month. Calculate how much less money for you this amounts to.

What would you have to change in your life to avoid taking on any additional debt obligations? Name some categories where you can likely cut down on some expenses based on your current spending habits:

- ☐ Entertainment
- ☐ Groceries
- ☐ Restaurants
- ☐ Transportation
- ☐ Vacations
- ☐ Can you think of any other areas?

Now, can you apply your strategy to your real-life spending for a month and put away that 10% toward your savings? Can you keep it up for two months?

CHAPTER 6

The Interaction Of Your Minimalist Budget With Your Family And Friends

This chapter addresses the potential positive and negative aspects of the role your partner, kids, and friends can play in your minimalist budget approach. It's important to keep in mind that the lifestyle changes driven by your minimalist budget are likely to impact other people. This can be either a positive or negative effect. While you should not care what strangers think about your budget strategies, the people who are significant in your life can be important factors for your minimalist budget.

Partner / Spouse / Significant Other

Combining personal finances can be a challenge in a relationship. There are a lot of choices to make about how each person will contribute financially, and what the spending priorities and goals are.

If you have a jointly-owned budget with your significant other, it's critical that you have mutual understanding and support in your budgeting strategy. Shared goals and shared financial information are important to achieving your financial goals.

If you have not already, start with discussing your financial goals and come to a general consensus on your priorities. Some of the topics to cover in your discussion are:

- Where do you both see yourself financially in five, ten, twenty years?
- What kind of lifestyle do you envision now, and in the future, for your life together? Does one of you want to retire early, and the other would like to work longer but wants to go on some vacations?
- If you are just starting out with sharing your financial goals, how do you want to handle personal debt, credit card balances, student loans, and other obligations? Do they need to be comprehended into your combined spending and saving plan?
- Do you prefer to assign each partner to specific categories within the budget (i.e., one person would be responsible for living expenses, and the other one would focus on debt repayment and savings), or how would the responsibilities be shared?
- If your incomes are very different, does this have an impact on how you approach your banking and do you need a plan for properly recognizing each person's financial contributions? These can be very personal choices.

Your discussion should make it clear to both of you which aspect of your finances you are combining, and which ones you will keep separated. For example, you can allocate shared financial responsibility to some expenses, while retaining some money for discretionary spending. If you are living together but are not married, your shared budget should include at least your household expenses. It's not typical to share credit cards and bank accounts before being married, and even after getting married, this can be a highly personal choice.

When you create your minimalist budget together, the overall process is the same as what is involved in creating a personal budget: you need to define your income, basic living expenses, and financial goals, and then create a spending allocation that is consistent with your priorities and resources. For shared budgets, the areas that will be most impacted by differences in opinions will be savings allocation and discretionary spending. However, keep in mind that lifestyle choices will also impact your basic, non-negotiable expenses – for example, deciding on the size of the house you want to live in will impact your housing expenses.

Of course, consensus on everything is nice but hardly realistic. When there is a difference between yours and your partner's opinions (and there will be), it comes back to one of the basic concepts of a relationship: compromise. There is no formula for this, but in general, both of you will have to make tradeoffs.

A shared minimalist budget has to meet your individual needs and preferences. Perhaps you can alternate months on how to allocate your discretionary spending. You can also agree to temporarily or permanently reduce some expenses in favor of the others: if one of you likes to eat at nice restaurants, and the other one wants a vacation, cutting back on restaurant spending will be required, but you can both enjoy the vacation together.

You will also have to make choices that are personal, and there are no right answers. If your incomes are unequal (and chances are, that's the case), you can assign financial obligations and discretionary spending amounts that are proportional to each person's income. For example, each person would contribute 10% of their income to savings, and 10% of their income would be completely up to them how to spend. You can also assign specific categories of expenses to each person – for example; the grocery budget goes to the person who is most frequently buying the groceries.

The weekly budget reviews discussed in Chapter 3 are a great tool for measuring and communicating your financial performance when you are sharing a budget with someone else. This is the time to jointly plan and review your financial standings, discuss trade offs, and agree on compromises. Ensure that any issues are communicated clearly and calmly and that you both are in agreement on the issue remediation strategy. The budget reviews are not a complaining or blaming session – rather, you both need to determine what factors you can control and what each of you can contribute to achieving common goals.

In addition to regular budget reviews, another useful tool for organizing a shared financial life is using a budgeting app that you can both access on your phones. Such an app will allow you to quickly review your actual spending versus targets in various categories and track the status of your bill payments and other obligations. If both of you are diligent about updating and reviewing the info in your budgeting app, it can be a great communication and visualization tool for your financial accomplishments, as well as areas where you had to compromise.

An important aspect to keep in mind that the goal in compromising for your minimalist budget is not to keep everything even: this for that, "*I deserve to buy a new watch if you get to have a new phone.*" Instead, it's about agreeing on what really brings fulfillment into your shared life, what makes you happy, together, in the most financially-effective way possible. Sometimes, accumulating things or looking for things to buy is a distraction in a relationship. Once you stop chasing after "stuff," you and your partner may find that the simpler, goal-oriented life brings you closer together.

However, if you find that you frequently cannot come to an agreement on your budgeting strategy and its implementation, you may need to address underlying relationship issues. This may involve discussing your basic goals and motivations in further detail or seeking professional counseling. On the other hand, if you can generally come to an agreement on goals and priorities, but struggle with the complexities of actually making a combined budget, you can seek help from a financial planner or get advice from an objective third party.

When you live on a minimalist budget, make a distinction between spending consciously and conscious spending. You and your spouse may be very aware of your own and each other's spending – that's spending consciously. Spending consciously may make you and your spouse feel guilty about your purchases. It can even create conflict, as it may induce feelings of being judged or being compared to one another. Spending consciously may not necessarily reduce your spending, but conscious spending can. Conscious spending implies being purposeful about how you allocate your money, which is the underlying notion of minimalist budgeting. Your strategy should not involve making each other feel bad about spending money – quite the opposite, minimalist budgeting is about finding happiness and meaning in putting your money toward accomplishing your goals.

Discussing financial goals and spending motivations can become a powerful tool in getting to know more about your partner and achieving a new closeness. There is a reason why we value certain things, plan (or fail to plan) our spending and saving – perhaps it's the values we were raised with or something we have learned from our parents through their mistakes or life experiences that have shaped our financial habits. Getting to know your partner's motivations and coming to a consensus on goals and strategies can help you with strengthening both your financial position and your relationship.

Kids

Sharing your expenses and budgeting with your significant other can add complexity to your strategy. Sharing a budget with a family that includes kids can be even more challenging! But as we have learned, the concept of minimalism is about making things simpler and putting your time and resources toward the things you really want in life. A minimalist budget can help your family spend more time together in a rewarding way, and not focus so much on acquiring things.

While walking back to my car at a rest area one time, I saw an unusual scene. A couple and their four young kids were on the grassy part of the rest area, and the father was leading them on an exercise of doing jumping jacks. It looked like a very happy scene, with both the kids and adults smiling and laughing and little ones trying their best to imitate the older ones in the exercise. It was such a simple and amazing idea, to do something together with your kids, which is fun, free, does not require any special equipment, and is a good way to stretch out on a long road trip. All this, while kids in nearby cars were busy looking at their electronics, with the kids and parents mostly ignoring each other.

In a way, that scene symbolizes the minimalist budget approach – it shows that you do not have to spend money to enjoy life and have a great time with those who matter in your life. You can take a simple activity and substitute it in place of the clutter of electronics, snacks, and searching for the next thing to buy, which often consumes not just our lives, but our kids' lives too.

You can be doing your child a great favor by demonstrating that less can be more, that getting more stuff is not necessarily the key to happiness. There are several ways you can expose your kids in your minimalist budget approach and help them participate in it. Of course, some children are just too young to understand the concept of money, or that there is a finite amount of it you can have (even some adults struggle with the latter!). Utilize the following strategies:

- Set an example: Your kids are good at observing you and getting a sense of your values in life. Are you purposeful in how you acquire things and about the possessions you have inside the house? How strongly are you attached to the things you own and your spending habits? Your priorities in this matter can be a strong influence on your kids' behavior in acquiring new toys and just wanting to buy things when you go somewhere.

- Communicate with your children: The details of the information you give your kids will depend on their age, of course, but even in very simple terms, you can explain the benefits of minimalist budgeting and your reason behind using it. As much as is feasible, discuss some of your spending options with your children. Try to make them understand that there are choices associated with getting things and doing activities. Older children may jump to far-reaching conclusions – that you are getting rid of all your possessions and discontinuing using money. Be clear and consistent about the ways your minimalist budget approach will affect your kids. As with most changes, it will take time and practice.

- Also as much as practical, make them actively participate in making choices about optional spending – while providing for their necessities, of course. See if would they rather have this toy or that one, go to an amusement park, or have a new game. Being an active participant in decisions allows your kids to understand early on that life is about choices. It also helps them to realize why you can't always agree to get them that latest gadget, or game, or candy at the checkout lane.

- Lower your kids' expectations for instant gratification: Just like adults, kids are exposed to a lot of advertisements that tell them what they should want next. Instead of enjoying the toys they already have, they are conditioned to want the next cool thing, which results in a lot of wanting, complaining, and even whining. Practice moderate giving in to the wanting of new things. It will take consistency, and it may take time, but your child will be happier in the long term by learning to want less.

- Simplify toys: Especially for really young children, toys do not have to be overly complicated. Instead of modern electronic toys, which are easily broken and require battery replacements, consider classic, old-fashioned toys. In addition to being more practical (and fun and educational), these are likely to be more cost-effective as well. Simple toys encourage children to use their creativity and imagination and to play cooperatively with their siblings or other children to put together a story or a game.

- Monitor and regulate exposure to advertisements: By simply watching TV with commercials, your children get conditioned to wanting more and more things, no matter what they already own. You can set limits on the amount of TV they watch or even eliminate TV altogether and substitute content without

48

advertisements – for example, shows from Amazon Video or Netflix.

- Many kids' rooms are simply overflowing with toys and clothes. There is no available storage space, and it's hard to determine what's actually being made use of. Having too many toys is not necessarily a good thing – children cannot process having too many options to choose from, and an overabundance of play choices can cause anxiety and stress. In addition, the clutter of too many toys and clothes makes it difficult to clean and organize. Review what your kids already own and simplify.

- The decluttering process can be adjusted to the child's age and personality. Older kids, in particular, will not want you to decide for them what they need and don't need. Depending on your child's age, you can involve them in deciding what they would like to keep and what can be donated or discarded. You can also look for things that haven't been used in a long time (have they been stored in the shed or the basement for months or even years?), or things that are broken, or clothing items that the child outgrew.

- Your child may be reluctant to let go of things, even if they are not being used. To make the process easier, you can declutter in stages – perhaps get rid of one toy per week, or designate a clean-up time once per month when a certain number of toys or clothing items have to be disposed of. Make sure to communicate the reasons for cleaning up and decluttering. Children can be very motivated to let go of their possessions if they know that their toy is going to be donated to a child in need.

- Point out the benefits of having implemented a simpler and decluttered lifestyle: Your children may not notice it on their own, but you can make some observations for them to note – for example, that their room is easier to clear and things are easier to find. A minimalist budget may also allow you to shift your resources toward something you can enjoy as a family – for example, a vacation that you could not afford before.

- It's hard to demonstrate decluttering your life if your children receive a lot of gifts from others. Discuss your minimalist strategy with friends and family members who give your child gifts and set rules in place about what is an appropriate amount. If someone wants to contribute more than the gifting limits you have set, you can suggest that they make a donation to your child's 529 (college savings) plan.

- Stick to your rules: If you have set a limit of gifts or implemented the One In, One Out rule (discussed in Chapter 4), make sure to follow up and stay consistent in how you enforce these rules.

- Be ok with saying "no": Kids are not known to be long-term thinkers. Many of their wants and (expressed) needs will end up being things they don't use. In addition to guiding their choices, you often have to limit their choices or stop the acquisition process altogether by just saying "no." The ability to say "no" also goes a long way with well-meaning adults in your life who want to give your kids hand-me-downs and gifts. Be able to decline, when needed, gracefully.
- Instead of toys, give the gift of your time: Cherished memories are not made with things – they are made by spending time together and enjoying each other's company. Instead of focusing on how much to spend on your child's toys, focus on how you can have a great time together, as a family. In your child's point of view, your love and attention are much better than any toy you can give them. The gift of a great experience is also something you can encourage others to give to your children instead of toys.

Here are some ideas on how to meaningfully contribute to your child's experiences and development, while taking away the focus on acquiring more things:

- Spend time outdoors: You can go hiking, fishing, mountain biking – find an activity that suits your child's preferences and interests.
- Build or repair something together: Whether you are handy with tools or not, having a project to which you can both contribute can be a great way to make memories together. This can be a car or bike repair and maintenance, a treehouse project, or repairing a broken toy.
- Take a class: This can be music, a sport (swimming or karate, for example), or a cooking class for kids. You can find a class you can take together with your child, or this can be a class where your children can spend time with their siblings and friends, or make new friends.
- Learn something new together (even without taking a class): You can try a new hobby – painting, sewing, or a new sport.
- Do arts and crafts: You can work on the same project as a team, or set a theme and show off your art skills to each other.
- Go to a venue: A movie, a play, a concert for kids, the zoo are all great places to enjoy the moment and build memories together.
- Make a meal or creative snacks: Use your imagination and have fun in the kitchen.

Children don't need you to fulfill their every wish to be happy. They need you to provide for their basic needs, and they need your love and attention. A minimalist budget household will take out the clutter out of your kids' lives, encourage them to use their imagination in play, and will curb the cycle of wanting more things. This way, you can focus on what really matters in life.

Friends and Acquaintances

Even if they don't directly impact your household income and spending, your friends and acquaintances can still play a very large role in either supporting or undermining your minimalist budget approach. Friends can be a great positive influence on your motivation, and they can become role models for your goals and budgeting strategy (as well as showing us what to avoid by setting a negative example!). On the other hand, friends and other people in your life can also encourage you to focus on spending and demotivate you in other ways, both intentionally and unintentionally.

There are a number of strategies for preventing overspending due to the influence of other people in your life:

- Use minimalist budgeting to prioritize your goals: If spending time with friends is important to you (and your activities together involve spending money), make an allocation in your budget for this. You will need to evaluate other spending areas and make compromises as needed, but this is what minimalist budgeting is about.

- Communicate: Let friends know if an activity they are suggesting is not within your budget. You can also discuss your spending goals and priorities, and explain your reasoning for implementing conscious spending in your life. Your friends should know that your behavior is not just about having insufficient funds to spend, and they should not interpret it as you not wanting to spend time with them.

- Be honest with yourself: If you are facing an impulse purchase while shopping with someone else, question your own motivations. Do you really like this item, or are you trying to make an impression, or are you just avoiding the awkwardness of putting the item back? Finding the real reason behind wanting to buy something can also help you to find the motivation to avoid the purchase.

- Look for alternatives: If you have a social pattern that frequently makes you spend money on going out, entertainment, or shopping for fun, try to focus on the aspect that really matters to you: spending time with friends. Think of how to focus on the experience aspect, and not on the buying aspect of enjoying time with others. You can suggest alternatives to your friends or brainstorm ideas together. The bonus chapter of this book contains some ideas for how to reduce entertainment-related costs.

- Remember your minimalist budget tools: If you are worried about overspending when going out with your friends, don't forget the option of bringing only cash with you to limit how much you can spend.
- Have an accountability partner: If you have trouble staying within your budget on your own, recruit a friend who will hold you accountable for your spending, and discourage you from impulsive purchases. You can use this as a strategy for shopping trips or while on vacation with a friend, or you can even have regular budget reviews together, which can serve as a motivation to stay on track.
- Participate only in activities that you can pay for and have an exit strategy: Social situations can get complicated when it comes to paying. First, plan ahead and participate in activities you can afford and can pay your fair share for. It is also helpful to have an exit strategy if you want to leave a social situation gracefully without spending too much: make backup plans, or ask a friend or family member to text you so you have a reason to leave.
- Limit comparisons: As discussed in Chapter 1, our spending habits can be fueled by considerations of what someone else already has. Focus on your own happiness and buying priorities. Sometimes it's easy to justify an expense because someone you know has the same thing. In addition to questioning whether you need to make that purchase in the first place, also try to look at expenses as a fraction of your income, before you compare what you spend to other people's spending.

Don't be quick to envy people. Everyone makes compromises in how they spend their time and money. The neighbor who just got a new car may be able to afford it by working long days and not spending any time with his family. The friend who just went on a fun island vacation may be drowning in debt. Remember that you are doing what's right for you and your finances and other people have different life circumstances.

- Curb your assumptions and expectations: Remember that everyone's priorities are different. Once you decide how you want to allocate your money, even if it's a very purposeful and efficient spending plan, your friends may have different priorities. Don't judge how others are choosing to spend their money. If you are deciding on a trip or activity together, make a plan that works for everyone's budget (or make a choice of whether you can participate or not).
- Be ok with saying "no": Even with the best of intentions, our friends and family can cause us to acquire things we don't need. Sometimes this involves a friend asking us to go on a spontaneous shopping trip or egging us on to make an unplanned purchase. At

other times, it is friends and relatives offering us free items when they move or clean out their house. Keep your own goals in mind and know how to decline offers that are not aligned with your own priorities.

- Become a role model yourself: By using a minimalist budget to simplify your life and work on accomplishing your goals, you can demonstrate the benefits of this approach to others. You may even set someone else onto the path of financial simplicity and mindfulness that a minimalist budget brings you.

End of Chapter Exercise

Think of what proportion of your discretionary purchases are directly or indirectly influenced by people you know:

- ☐ None or very few
- ☐ Some (less than 50%)
- ☐ A considerable amount (50% or more)
- ☐ Almost all

Are you investing both time and money into your relationships?

BONUS CHAPTER
Minimalist Budget Meets Frugality

As we discussed in Chapter 1, living on a minimalist budget is not the same thing as being frugal. However, there is an overlap between the two aspects. The same person may seek simplicity and purposefulness in their budget, at the same time as aiming to save money and make their dollar go further.

Many of us work very hard at finding the best deal for big purchases, but daily waste money on small items. Often, the small things are the ones that end up cluttering our lives and prevent us from being able to put away money toward achieving our goals. It's important to be consistent and use your minimalist mindset approach for all your purchases.

Examine your expenses and ask yourself whether each one is an efficient use of your money. The exact ways to organize and streamline your savings will depend on the specifics of everyone's personal situation. Consider the following ideas and ask yourself if you can come up with even better approaches for making the best use of your money.

Housing and Utilities

Most of us have a commitment to a rental agreement or a mortgage, so it's understandable that housing-related changes cannot be done lightly or quickly.

Here is what you can do in the short-term to make your spending on housing and utilities more efficient:

- Be mindful of your energy usage that can lead to higher utility bills. Heating and cooling the house is likely a major part of your utility expenses. A programmable thermostat can go a long way to simplifying how you control the temperature and avoid unnecessarily heating the house while you are not in it. As a free substitute for a programmable thermostat, you can also set reminders on your phone for changing the temperature before going to work or going to sleep.
- To further reduce your utility bills, consider energy-saving steps, such as using energy-efficient lightbulbs, making sure your window panes are properly insulated, turning down the water heater temperature, and unplugging electronics you are not using frequently. Energy-efficient fans can also be a great money-saving alternative to air conditioning.
- House maintenance items, such as changing your air conditioning filters and cleaning your vents can go a long way to extending the life of your air conditioning unit and saving you money in the long run.

- If you own your appliances and you have to replace one, pick an energy-efficient model that will save you money over time.
- If you own your home, regular home maintenance will help you avoid big repairs down the road. Critical maintenance items include properly servicing your water heater and septic tank, regularly cleaning your refrigerator coils, cleaning your AC unit and humidifier, and clearing the gutters. There are also many great resources online to help you reduce your utility costs and perform home maintenance.
- Investing in maintaining your home is a good thing, but be mindful of what home improvement projects you take on. The effort and money you put in needs to add value to your life. For example, if you are remodeling a room you barely use, ask yourself if you are getting the most value out of this spending, and does it make your life better.
- If you own your home, refinancing your mortgage to a lower rate can also save you money.
- If you have extra living space in your home, consider renting it out.
- If you are renting your home and your lease is coming up for renewal, negotiate a lower rental rate with your landlord. As part of your negotiation, you can offer to sign a longer lease term in exchange for a lower rate. You can also offer to do small maintenance tasks or give referrals to your landlord's other properties.

In the medium and long-term:

Consider whether the reason you live where you live still applies. Can you make your life simpler by moving to a different house/apartment or a different area altogether? For some people, house and lawn maintenance is something that brings joy to their life. For others, it's time- and money-consuming work, and moving to a housing arrangement where the association takes care of maintenance may greatly simplify their life.

Here are some options to consider and research. See if they may fit your minimalist budget better than your current housing choice:

- Downsize your house: If you are not using all the rooms in your house, they become a source of extra cleaning work and higher utility bills. Consider moving to a smaller house or apartment where you can fully utilize the available living space.
- Move to a less expensive area: If you live in the city, consider moving to the suburbs, where the cost of living is usually lower. You can also find an area with lower housing costs and lower property taxes. This can involve moving to a different neighborhood close to where you currently live, or if your job and

55

personal situation allows you to, you can look at moving to a different region, state, or even to a different country.

- Consider other housing options: If you live in a house, investigate moving to an apartment or condo where the association fees cover the lawn service and some of the maintenance. For some people, moving to a mobile home community has worked out as a great way to save money.
- In some situations, a great option for lowering housing costs is to move in to live with someone else and share living expenses. This can involve moving in with your parents, a friend, or a roommate.

Of course, these ideas may not fit all lifestyles and situations, but it's important that the place where you live (and into which, likely, a significant amount of your budget is going to) represents your minimalist budget mindset.

Cable/Phone Bill/Internet Bill/Other Service Subscriptions

Review the following items to ensure you are getting the most value from spending money on various service subscriptions:

- If you have a subscription to a streaming service, such as Netflix, Hulu, Amazon Video, Pandora, etc., review how much you actually use these services. Can you live without some of them? Are you willing to give it a try for a few months? Keep in mind; you can often get a month for free from a lot of these services, so canceling for a few months and then re-subscribing (if needed) will at least save you some money in the short-term. And you may find that you don't miss it that much after all.
- If you have subscribed to a service for a specific purpose that no longer applies (for example, to watch a specific show via a streaming service), cancel the subscription as soon as it has fulfilled its purpose.
- Keep track of your subscriptions. Making a list of each service that you have subscribed to and its respective cost can make you realize that you have a lot of savings opportunities in this area. In addition, review your subscription bills carefully. Especially when it comes to phone, internet, and cable bills, providers often add charges that they don't advertise with their initial offers. Make sure you know what you are paying for, and how much.
- Some subscription services, specifically those that physically deliver food or other items to your house, will allow you to skip a delivery. Utilize this option when you are out of town or just don't need the item during a specific week.

- Some subscriptions will give you discounts for referring other people to the service or for adding more users to the account. Make sure to take advantage of these savings opportunities.
- If you have a cell phone, this is likely one of your most expensive subscriptions. And higher data usage rates usually mean that you pay a higher subscription fee. Check your actual data usage – do you really need an unlimited data plan? Review the phone subscription packages your provider offers and check if your actual usage allows you to switch to a less expensive package.
- To reduce your data usage, utilize Wi-Fi as much as possible. You can also check for and limit the apps that are running in the background using up your data and your battery.
- Many cell phone carriers will give you a discount if you sign up for automatic payments or paperless billing – take advantage of this money-saving option.
- Depending on the terms of your contract, it may be useful to shop around and switch to a less expensive package with another provider. After you check competitor rates, you can also negotiate with your current provider to match the lower price.
- Don't be in a rush to get the latest phone. Keeping your current phone longer and buying an older model when you do have to replace it can save you a lot of money. In addition, you can avoid contract fees by not buying your phone from your service carrier – purchase a new or used no-contact phone. If you have friends who have to have the latest model, ask if you can buy their current phone when they upgrade.
- When it comes to saving money on your cable and internet subscriptions, shopping around for better deals and negotiating with your service provider can save you a lot of money. As a possible negotiation tactic, you can even cancel your service until you get a better offer from the service provider. Living without a cable or internet subscription for a month may sound impossible, but it's easier than you think with many businesses offering free Wi-Fi.
- You can also save on the cost of renting your internet router/modem. If you are being charged this fee, simply check what model router you have and purchase one – they are not very expensive. Once you return the equipment you were renting to the service provider, make sure that the rental cost is no longer on your bill.
- Cable is expensive, and there are many alternatives that can save you money. Depending on what you usually watch, you can look into substituting cable with streaming services, such as Netflix or Hulu, or a single-channel subscription, such as HBO. With

services like YouTube TV, you can still watch network television, and many networks make their content available for viewing via free apps, as well. With an inexpensive antenna, you can watch your local TV and HDTV for free. Don't forget that getting movies for free at the local library is an option, and the selection there can be better than on many cable channels!

- With all your subscriptions, be aware of what contracts and early termination fees you are signing up for. Sometimes paying an early termination fee makes sense to save money on the subscription itself, but this factor should be taken into account both when considering a new subscription, and when looking at unsubscribing from a service. In addition, be aware of any applicable data limits and other conditions that can cost you a lot more money than what you thought you were going to pay.
- Most importantly, ask yourself if your subscriptions are really adding value to your life and making you happy. Can you find alternatives that are free or do not cost as much?

Groceries

- For grocery shopping, make a plan, and buy only what you need. Most of us throw out a surprisingly large proportion of the food we buy (or it's still in an expired state in your refrigerator, and you are just not throwing it out). Follow this process when going shopping for food:
  - o Before going to the store, decide how many days you are buying food for (how many meals are you making?).
  - o Make a list of the perishable things you need for this many days. Note that this does not have to be specific things – you can list categories of items such as "main dish meat," "salad ingredients," "sides," and purchase them depending on what is on sale or looks freshest. Less perishable items like olive oil should make it to the list when you are running low on those.
  - o Stick to this list when you are shopping – no impulse purchases!
  - o Toward the end of the number of days you have shopped for, check how useful your list was – did you run out of anything too early, or end up with too much of something? Adjust your next shopping list accordingly.
- Check your refrigerator, freezer, and pantry for items you already have, before going grocery shopping. Can you use some of what you already have as part of your ingredients? Challenge yourself and your family to make a meal plan that will use up your existing

food items before they expire – you can be creative or look up recipes online by searching for ones with specific ingredients.

- While shopping for groceries, it helps to track your total, either using your phone's calculator or rounding up the price and making tally marks on a piece of paper. This way, you avoid bad surprises at the checkout, and knowing the total helps you to make purchasing decisions as you go. If you often end up with a grocery total that's higher than what you budgeted, use the "cash only" strategy – leave your credit card at home and bring what you intend to spend in cash. You may have to decide which items to put back, but being on a budget requires compromises.

- Don't buy more groceries than you need, especially when it comes to perishable food. Sale offers often induce us to buy a higher quantity (for example, via "buy one, get one free" or 5 for $10 deals). Keep in mind that in most stores, the same discounted price applies even if you buy just one item. At warehouse clubs such as Sam's Club or Costco, buying in bulk can save you money, but only if you actually use all of what you purchase.

- On the other hand, if there are less perishable items you buy consistently, stock up when these items are on sale.

- Buy ingredients you can re-use across multiple meals, and avoid items that can only be used for a specific dish. To save time and money, buy enough items to make a big meal, and use what's left over for lunch or other meals later in the week.

- Also, to save both time and money, consider the option of shopping online and picking up your order at the grocery store. This helps you to avoid impulse purchases, and you can easily review the available deals to select the items you want to buy.

- Check for deals at other grocery stores. You may have picked where you shop based on the store's location, quality, selection, or prices, but don't overlook what other stores can offer you, even if you have to drive a little farther.

- Simplify your meals. A delicious dinner does not have to have a lot of ingredients or require a long time to prepare. Look up quick and simple recipes – you will spend less time on grocery shopping and cooking and have more time to enjoy other things.

- Try generic brands or brands owned by the grocery store. These often use the same ingredients as brand names but are less expensive because they are more cost-effective for the grocery store.

- Buy fruits and vegetables that are in season. They are less expensive, fresher, and taste better than out of season produce that has been shipped in from a long distance away. You can also check the country of origin of the produce to get an idea of how far it had to travel to get to your store.

- Be selective about who you go to the grocery store with. Our friends or spouse can influence us to make impulse purchases or buy more than how much we actually need. If you go grocery shopping with kids, set strict rules about the items you intend to purchase and stick with the limits you set.
- Don't go shopping for groceries when you are hungry (and, from the advice above, don't bring people who are hungry with you). You will end up buying more than you planned on because your wants start to feel more like your needs when you are hungry.

Restaurants

Restaurant expenses can be high, compared to grocery shopping. For some, eating out simplifies their life or adds value to their life by being a reason to spend time with friends and family, and that's just fine. For others, eating out is a device to compensate for ineffective grocery trip planning.

As part of your minimalist budget planning, it's important to consider the amounts you spend on groceries and eating out, as well as how they compare to each other. Ask yourself if more effective grocery planning would reduce the need for eating out at restaurants. If your reason for eating out at restaurants is mostly to spend time with friends and family, consider whether simpler alternatives would also fulfill the same purpose – for example, making a meal together at home, meeting up at a bookstore, going for a walk together. If you do decide to go out to a restaurant, consider these tips for saving money:

- Look for special offers. A lot of restaurants have rotating deals, such as free appetizers when you buy a meal, or a "kids eat free" day. There are many restaurants that will treat you to a free meal, drink, or dessert for your birthday. You can also take advantage of coupons and offers in the local paper, ads that come to your house, or discounts on websites such as Groupon.
- Get discounted gift cards for restaurants. Individual restaurants sometimes sell discounted gift cards on their websites. In addition, you can get discounts on websites, such as restaurants.com and in warehouse clubs.
- Going to a restaurant can give you an opportunity to have a unique meal that you would not necessarily want to, or be able to cook at home. Take advantage of this and try items that you would not cook yourself – otherwise, you could have saved money by making the same meal at home.
- Be aware of how much you spend on beverages and consider drinking water instead. Beverages at restaurants are usually

overpriced compared to enjoying the same carbonated drinks or beer at home after buying it from a grocery store. Limit your beverage purchases at restaurants to what actually enhances the meal – such as a wine that pairs with a certain dish. Otherwise, drink water – it will also enable you to enjoy the flavor of your food better.

- Same as with beverages, desserts at restaurants are often overpriced. Skip the dessert at the restaurant, and if you still want something sweet when you get home, have ice cream or another frozen dessert option available for this purpose. Frozen desserts can usually be kept for a long time, so they are more practical than buying pastries for this purpose.
- Getting your meal to go can be a great money-saving option, as you can save on the tip and prepare your own salad or other add-ons.
- Order only an appetizer or split an entrée with another person. Restaurants often give us a lot more food than we can eat, and taking leftovers with you is not always the convenient or practical option. Try ordering just an appetizer and see if you still feel hungry after eating it. You can also order one meal to share between two people, or one meal and one appetizer. You will often find that this is quite enough food.
- If you do get a meal that's too much for you to eat, stop eating as soon as you are starting to feel full and ask for a container to take it to go.
- Going out to a restaurant for lunch instead of dinner is also a good option: lunch prices are typically lower, and portions are smaller, so it's easier on your wallet and your stomach.
- Don't assume that a "special" is a good deal. Specials are often experimental recipes or dishes made with an item that the restaurant has too much of. Check what the "special" price is and make a comparison against your other options.
- Eating at a restaurant should not be your "go-to" option for getting food. Restaurants are both more expensive than making meals at home, and they often offer poor nutritional value compared to what you would choose if cooking. Limit your restaurant meals to special occasions, and look for more practical alternatives if you eat at restaurants to socialize.
- Impulse snack and beverage purchases can cut into your budget plans. When you review your spending, make sure that you are aware of the amount you spend on this category — question whether you could have spent the same money in a better way. You can either incorporate these purchases into your planned

budget (and stick to your decision) or make a conscious decision to plan your meals in a more effective way.

- Keep in mind that cheap food is not necessarily better for your budget in the long term if it lacks nutrition and ends up causing health issues. At the same time, a very expensive meal at a restaurant may not be great for your health, either. Be purposeful about choosing the food you eat and how you purchase it.

Transportation

Simplifying your transportation costs depends largely on your life situation – what your lifestyle and family needs are, whether you live in an urban, suburban, or rural area. Some changes may be easy to implement, while others will require time and lifestyle adjustments. Here are some of the ways you can reduce your transportation-related costs:

- Consider what vehicles you own and why you own them. Similar to housing, changing your car or downsizing from several cars to one for the household can be an important decision with lasting consequences. Review your vehicle usage (how often do you actually use it, do you need the size, towing capacity, luxury accessories, etc.). Also, review your financial obligations for the vehicles you own (the amount and duration of lease payments or loan payments). Take into account items that may be costing you money unnecessarily or complicating your life: maintenance and repair costs, car insurance, fuel cost, parking fees. Decide if you can make your life simpler and more financially practical, by either changing the kind of car you have or eliminating a vehicle you own from your life altogether.
- Perform regular maintenance on your vehicle. This will save you money by reducing the number of breakdowns and other unexpected expenses, which could be much more costly than maintenance. Even a simple thing like maintaining the proper pressure in your tires can save you money on fuel costs (not to mention increasing your driving safety). Using only the recommended grade of octane is also important, as this is the fuel your car was designed to work with.
- Instead of owning two or more vehicles in your household, consider downsizing to just one and make an arrangement where one of you is the "chauffeur," or you and your spouse can take turns giving each other rides to work.
- Don't speed and obey driving laws. Speeding and parking tickets can be expensive. In addition to costing you money, speeding and other driving violations can also endanger people's lives. Driving sensibly (not speeding and not driving aggressively) will also improve your fuel economy and save you money on fuel costs.

- Other ways to reduce your fuel costs include getting a credit card that gives you cash back on gasoline purchases or buying fuel from a store chain that offers discounted fuel prices to members.
- Make smart purchasing decisions and shop around. When you are looking to buy a new vehicle, parts, or car insurance, make sure to do your research, so you are getting good value for your money. When buying a vehicle, in addition to considering the price of the car itself, also make sure to evaluate maintenance, insurance, fuel consumption, and other costs of ownership.
- If you are financing a car, compare rates from multiple financial organizations. Unless you are receiving a 0% interest rate, put down the largest down payment you can afford, to reduce the amount of interest you will pay.
- When buying car insurance, review what coverage you actually need and don't select coverage options just because they are offered. If you are a good driver, it may also make sense to choose coverage with a high deductible – it will save you money on monthly premiums, although it will cost you more if you have an accident. In addition, check the discounts offered by the insurance provider. You can get a discount by being a part of an affinity group, taking a defensive driving course, having a good driving record, or combining your insurance coverages (home, life, and auto) into one provider.
- Go eco-friendly. Walk or use a bicycle when you can. This is good for your wallet, your health, and for the environment. If you drive somewhere that involves multiple destinations, consider parking your car somewhere that allows you to access more than one destination on foot.
- When possible, use public transportation. This will allow you to save money on fuel, parking fees, and to reduce the wear and tear on the vehicles you own. If you have sufficient public transportation options, you can even avoid owning a vehicle altogether, allowing you to save further on vehicle insurance and maintenance.
- If you need a vehicle infrequently, consider renting one when you need it, or signing up for a car share network. Same as with public transportation, this will let you avoid the cost of vehicle ownership.
- To save money on public transportation, taxis, and ride-sharing services, examine how much you spend per month on this type of expense. Decide if you can make your life simpler by walking, riding a bike, or sharing rides with others.
- To save on transportation while traveling, consider multiple options of how to get to your destination. For example, buses can

save you money compared to air travel, and they can get you to remote destinations that commercial airlines don't service. When you do fly, consider various route options, as flying through an airline hub city or taking connecting flights can save you money.

A final note to simplifying your transportation budget: analyze not only how you can reduce or simplify the transportation expense itself, but also the reason for why you are making the trips in the first place. For a week or so, write down the places you are going to and then review the overall picture of your travels. Are there any trips you can combine, and are all the trips done for something that brings value and purpose to your life? Are there other activities you can do that involve shorter or fewer trips but still fulfill the purpose?

Clothes and Personal Care

Clothes and personal care are important categories where you have to make distinctions between your wants and needs. The decision is personal – things like the latest fashion, massages, manicures, and expensive health care products may be extremely important to some and not at all important to others (and there is a spectrum of everyone in between).

This is one of the categories that most clearly distinguish a frugal approach from a minimalist approach. With a frugal approach, you would simply cut out most expenses in this category, except buying simple clothes you must have to function and maintaining basic hygiene. With a minimalist budget approach, you can decide how important the things in this category are to you and make tradeoffs with other categories. If you put a value on having a new outfit every month, you can put less value on eating out or going on a vacation. However, as with every expense on your list, you must ask yourself if the expenses in this category are really adding value and happiness to your life. Are you willing to sacrifice them for something more important, or reduce the frequency of making these purchases?

You can use the following techniques to save money on clothes and personal care:

- Before you go shopping for new clothes, review your current wardrobe and donate what you don't wear or sell the items to consignment stores. To minimize adding clutter to your life, you can implement the "one in, one out" rule described in Chapter 4. You can also trade the clothes you don't use with friends and family.
- When you do go shopping for new clothes, use the same techniques as for grocery shopping: make a list and stick to it, and if you think you might make impulse purchases, bring only enough cash to spend the amount you intend.

- Consider the cleaning costs when you buy new items. Dry cleaning costs can add up if you have a lot of clothes that require it. In addition, you may become hesitant to wear something if it's too difficult to clean, resulting in an expensive item doing nothing in your closet.
- Take care of your clothing and follow the care instructions on the tags. It's not money well spent if a piece of clothing gets ruined the first time you wash it.
- Buy out of season to take advantage of sales and steep discounts.
- Don't overlook thrift stores. In addition to selling deeply discounted gently used clothing, thrift stores also sell new items, with tags, that others have donated. Thrift stores can be especially useful if you are looking for a piece of clothing to wear for a one-time occasion or to experiment with a new style.
- Even if you enjoy wearing expensive name brand products, consider buying your basic clothes – socks, t-shirts to wear under shirts, tank tops – from inexpensive stores.
- Focus on simple and functional – trendy clothes are quickly out of style, and do you really have to make a fashion statement while working out?
- Saving on personal care items, such as toiletries or makeup, involves combining some of the techniques for saving on groceries and clothes: examine what you already own and use it up before buying new things. When you do buy, since most personal care items have a relatively long shelf life, try to buy in bulk when possible to save money, but check the expiration dates to make sure you can use it up in time. While expensive name brand products may be important to you for some items, consider using generic brands when possible. As with any purchase, ask yourself if the item you are buying is really serving a purpose in your life.

Health Insurance and Medical Expenses

In most cases, we do not get to pick our health conditions and how much they cost to manage, so medical expenses are difficult to reduce or simplify. However, there are still several things you can do to ensure that your approach to health-related spending is in line with your minimalist budget. To simplify and reduce your health care and medical expenses, consider the following:
- Review your health plan to make sure it's right for the number of your medical expenses and any specific medical condition coverage that you need. Make sure you understand your health benefits, what is covered, and what the copayments and deductibles are:

- If you are in relatively good health and have a health insurance policy (and have some decision-making power over what type of insurance it is), consider switching to a high-deductible policy. This will lower your monthly insurance costs. You can put away the extra money toward savings, which can be used toward the deductible if needed.
- If you have health issues that need treatment, a health plan with higher premiums and more coverage is appropriate. You should also compare prescription drug coverage among health care plans.
- If you have a spouse, check if it's more cost-effective for one of you to be covered by the other's insurance under a family plan.
- Seek work that provides health insurance coverage or assistance.
- Research medical cost-sharing networks that you may qualify for. These can save you a significant amount of money, and they can be based on your faith, professional affiliation, and other qualifications.
- If you take medications, ask your doctor if you can switch to generic medicines or less expensive medicines that can treat the same condition. You can also ask for free medication samples. Don't neglect to take your prescribed medicines, as this can cause additional health issues and health care expenses.
- Get routine health exams and health screenings – these can detect issues that will cause significant health problems and expenses down the road, so you can take preventative and corrective action now.
- Have an emergency fund. Even with good health care coverage, you may have to deal with deductibles and expenses that are not covered by health insurance. Make sure you have money set aside to spend on emergencies, as well as to cover for any lost income if you are unable to work.
- Avoid the emergency room for non-life-threatening issues. Go to your doctor or a walk-in clinic when it's not an emergency – this is much more cost effective and wait times at a walk-in clinic are often lower than at the ER.
- Use a Health Care Savings Account (HSA) or Flexible Spending Account (FSA). These are savings accounts that allow you to deposit pre-tax money, as long as you use them for medical-related expenses. Because the money is not taxed, your dollar can go a lot further by using these accounts.
- When you get a medical bill, review it carefully to make sure you understand all the charges and there are not any errors in the billing. If you cannot afford to pay the bill, you can often negotiate

the cost with the medical provider or get a low-interest payment plan.

- As one of the most important but often overlooked strategies - take care of your health! That's a topic for a whole other book (or a thousand of them), but the benefits of living healthy is a great investment into reducing your health care costs, improving your outlook on life, and allowing you to lead a life where you are able to do things that make you happy.

Entertainment

If you are used to expensive activities to entertain you, you may have developed an association between fun and spending money. But activities do not have to be expensive to be fun – in fact, living on a minimalist budget will help you realize that fun can be found in simple things.

Think of the activities you do now for entertainment and decide how well they fit in your budget. If you are enjoying what you are doing now – great. However, it's important to consider the opportunity cost of your activities – both from financial and time investment perspectives. Opportunity cost means you are no longer able to spend this money, and this time on something else.

Make a list of simple and inexpensive entertainment activities you might enjoy in place of your current ones. Here are some suggestions and thought starters:

- There are a number of ways to save money when you go out to a restaurant for entertainment. See the "Restaurants" section of this chapter for some ideas on this topic.
- If you like going out for drinks for entertainment, save money by going at "happy hour," which most bars offer. You can also check for special deals and events at your local establishments.
- If you enjoy going to sports venues, attend a local or an amateur game instead of a professional one. High school and college games, as well as minor league games, can often be attended for just a fraction of the price of seeing a professional team play.
- Many nature-related activities are free or inexpensive. If you have a park nearby, you can go for a hike, ride a bike, or rent a canoe or kayak. You can also observe wildlife, go bird watching, or use nature as your inspiration for another hobby such as painting or photography.
- If you enjoy movies, you probably know that movie theaters are very expensive. Save money by attending a matinee (early afternoon showtime), or by going to an independent film theater, where the prices are lower. You can also rent movies for free from a public library, or rent them very inexpensively from Redbox.

- If you enjoy attending live music events, search online for free concerts in your area. There are regular events in most major cities. You can also look for live music performances at local bars and coffee shops.
- If you enjoy reading, there are a number of ways to read the content that interests you for free. There are always public libraries, some even offering digital books you can check out. Many information sources on the internet are free – news publications, how-to blogs, travel journals. You can also find many free digital books online – for example, on sites like Project Gutenberg and ManyBooks.net. If you read a lot, you can also join Kindle Unlimited, which offers a huge amount of free titles for a small monthly fee plus a free trial.
- Take a class or attend a lecture. Many organizations and community establishments offer free or inexpensive classes to both adults and children. You can learn about cooking, painting, photography, a new sport, and many other topics. Some home improvement stores offer DIY classes, which can help you save money on home repairs. You can also use a class as an opportunity to spend time with friends and family or to meet new people.
- Volunteer for a cause that interests you. You can use your time to improve your community and help people and animals. By volunteering at events, you also get to attend the event for free.
- If you find yourself with a lot of spare time on your hands, also consider this time as an opportunity to make money. You can look for a gig or a side job on places like Craigslist or Indeed.com. If you have a hobby, think of ways you can turn that hobby into profit – by selling something that you make, or by working as a coach or consultant for people who would like to learn your skills.
- There are many ways to spend time with friends and family that don't involve going out to restaurants or expensive venues. You can organize a barbeque or a game night, play board games, play sports, or pick some of the suggestions on this list and do them together.

As discussed earlier, in deciding on purchases in the entertainment category, focus on buying experiences rather than things. Physical objects tend to clutter your life and may not add much value to it unless you use them frequently. Experiences are something that you can remember and share with others, something that can deepen a relationship and make a positive impact on you as a person.

Focusing on experiences and consumable items is also a good approach when purchasing someone else a gift. You will avoid adding clutter to someone else's life and instead give them a nice experience. Giving someone gourmet coffee, fancy candy, a gift card for a movie theater or a spa can make for a thoughtful gift and will certainly be appreciated more than an object that they may or may not use.

End of Chapter Exercise

Imagine you just won $1000 (after taxes).
What would you do with this money?

- ☐ Put it toward your current bills and debt obligations
- ☐ Save it for a rainy day
- ☐ Buy yourself something nice or plan a vacation
- ☐ Donate it or give it to someone else
- ☐ Save it in a retirement account

There is no right answer to this question. Examine your answer for how well it aligns with your own values and with what you have learned about the concept of minimalist budgeting.

CONCLUSION

There are trade offs in life, and you have to make a conscious decision about how you want to spend your money. Using a minimalist budget is not about depriving yourself. Rather, it is about differentiating between your needs and your indulgences and cutting out unnecessary expenses and clutter from your life. It's about prioritizing what you want in life and directing your money to where it will matter most, instead of spending it on trivial things that don't matter. A minimalist budget allows you to assess how much money you have coming in and going out, and how to align this cash flow to your goals in life.

The exact implementation of the minimalist budget concepts described in this book will vary for everyone. We all come from different life situations and financial backgrounds. We all have different priorities and things we value. But the principles guiding minimalist budgeting are applicable to any level of income and with a wide variety of financial goals.

Living on a minimalist budget can be an incredibly powerful tool for your life. It uses intentionality and decision-making as a path to finding contentment and accomplishing your financial goals.

Thank you so much for making it through to the end of this book. I hope it was informative and able to provide you with all of the tools you need for your Minimalist Budget journey. The next step is to start trying these techniques and find out what works best for you. Lastly, if you enjoyed this book, I ask that you please take the time to rate it on Amazon. Your honest review would be greatly appreciated. Thank you!

DESCRIPTION

This book is an informative and comprehensive guide to minimalist budgeting. It introduces you to the concept of a minimalist budget, explains the strategies and techniques associated with it, and teaches you how to apply minimalist budgeting in everyday life.

The first chapter of this book explains what a minimalist budget is about and also what it's not. This part of the book discusses how a minimalist budget can improve your life, and how critical your mindset and attitude are to your minimalist budget approach.

In chapter two, you will learn how to define your financial goals and priorities. In addition, this chapter discusses how to find motivation and inspiration to follow through with your minimalist budget goals.

In chapter three, you will learn about specific steps to create, implement, and maintain your own minimalist budget.

Chapter four provides you with a toolbox of minimalist budget tools, as well as tips and tricks to make budgeting easier and more effective.

Chapter five discusses how to deal with financial setbacks and changes that you may experience while following the minimalist budget. This part will also help you with controlling compulsive spending and establishing new, positive habits.

In chapter six, you will learn how your partner, kids, and friends can play a role in your minimalist budget approach. Both positive and negative aspects of this interaction will be discussed. This chapter also shows how a minimalist budget can positively impact your relationships and vice versa.

The bonus chapter offers you specific strategies and ways to save money in various categories of expenses, all while helping you to simplify your financial life and reduce clutter in your possessions.

At the end of each chapter, you have an opportunity to apply what you have learned to your own life through a simple exercise.

After reading this book, you will have a good understanding of minimalist budgeting and practical approaches to applying it to your life.